Young Writers

The Big
Poetry Machine

West Country Poets

Edited by Lisa Adlam

First published in Great Britain in 2009 by:

Young Writers
Remus House
Coltsfoot Drive
Peterborough
PE2 9JX
Telephone: 01733 890066
Website: www.youngwriters.co.uk

Book Design by Spencer Hart & Tim Christian

SB ISBN 978-1-84431-977-0

Foreword

Young Writers' Big Green Poetry Machine is a showcase for our nation's most brilliant young poets to share their thoughts, hopes and fears for the planet they call home.

Young Writers was established in 1991 to nurture creativity in our children and young adults, to give them an interest in poetry and an outlet to express themselves. Seeing their work in print will encourage them to keep writing as they grow, and become our poets of tomorrow.

Selecting the poems has been challenging and immensely rewarding. The effort and imagination invested by these young writers makes their poems a pleasure to enjoy reading time and time again.

Contents

Milverton CP School, Taunton

Sharpness Primary School, Berkeley

Windwhistle Primary School, Weston-super-Mare

The Poems

Help The Homeless

Dirty woman on the streets,
In her heart she feels sorrow,
People sniping can be heard,
She wishes for tomorrow.
But tomorrow will be just the same,
That will be for sure,
She's still homeless on the street,
She's heard it all before.
She feels like she's invisible,
Being thought of badly,
She wishes she could have a home,
She'd settle for that gladly.
Clothes are torn, hair all straggly,
Shoes are far too small,
Blisters all over her feet,
She despises them all.
I am sure she needs some nice warm clothes,
And lots of money to spend,
But all she really wants in life,
Is one special friend.

Alice Fisher (11)
Ann Edwards Primary School, Cirencester

Destruction

A bullet flies through the air,
While others lounge upon a chair,
An innocent man falls dead on the floor,
Blood seeping into the field of war.

In a rainforest across the world,
A waking sloth does uncurl,
To find himself moving towards the ground.
This sloth's home will be sold for a pound,
Faster animals and quicker birds scatter,
But this poor sloth to us doesn't matter.

Somewhere else, quite far away,
Choking smoke drifts into a bay,
There it rises into the sky,
Burning a hole above us, why?

A mother bear, a polar bear,
Stands with her baby taking good care,
Then with a crack, like a snap of a twig,
The ice breaks in two but the ocean's too big.
Mother's child floats out of the bay,
The problem worsens every day.

Would you ever think
That the world's on the brink,
Because of one race,
Called humans?

Lucy Stephenson (10)
Ann Edwards Primary School, Cirencester

Pollution

The sky is black with an evil cloak of darkness,
hugging the blue sky and not letting go.

A drop of litter can damage a beautiful swan,
just a bit of rubbish in the bin can save the lives of many.

The trees are screaming and crying as they are being hacked down
by men in bright yellow hats, wielding monstrous chainsaws.

The gorillas' homes are being ripped to pieces,
and soon they will end up like the trees.

The fish cannot survive in polluted water,
when tons of rubbish are being selfishly dumped into the pond.

The hole in the ozone layer is getting bigger and bigger,
and the days are getting hotter.

The icebergs are melting and it won't be long,
until the polar bear disappears like the gorilla.

Big factories are giving off smoke into the air,
and in a few years it will disappear like the polar bear.

Charlie Price (10)
Ann Edwards Primary School, Cirencester

An Awful War

There is a war,
An awful war,
With rifle guns firing,
And man after man dying,
With the loss of loved ones' lives,
Blood scattered along a path,
A path of life or death,
Which soldiers must take.
Step by step they think of sadness,
The sadness of not being at home,
With their loving families.
We should think about them each day,
And try to embrace,
The sorrow and pain
Of those poor soldiers,
Who died for their country that day.

Jemma Bobe (10)
Ann Edwards Primary School, Cirencester

Black Nature

They have no voice but the wind,
No defence but the birds,
All because of Man's sin,
Thinking of only themselves.

Rabbits sprint away,
As trees fall to the ground,
Woodpeckers close their eyes,
Never forget that cracking sound.

Black clouds loom above the forests,
And chainsaws destroy at will.
A monstrous curse for the pennies in Man's purse,
A precious thing to kill.

Matthew David Isles (10)
Ann Edwards Primary School, Cirencester

Environmentally Friendly

People take life so easy,
Open the door to show me,
It isn't fair,
We must repair
The damage that we've done,
It can be so much fun.
If we do it together,
We can look after the world forever.
It's our lives we'll spare,
We need to take more care,
If we don't act fast,
This world will be the past.

Jago Hartland (11)
Ann Edwards Primary School, Cirencester

Environment Poem

It's about time we should save this world,
For my friends, family and animals.
It's just not fair,
For some don't care,
The unmistakable damage that we've done,
So when you are ill at home one day, lying there in bed,
Think of the sickly world,
For you may get better that day,
But ask yourself this question,
About our planet's health,
Will the world ever be the same again?

Charlotte Nelson-Robins (11)
Ann Edwards Primary School, Cirencester

Chaos In The Forest

Fire raging in gorillas' hearts,
They see smoke rise as the forest burns down,
Their home is a wasteland because of Man's sin,
Pain and misery spread along the ground,
All they hear is the crash of homes,
Lives are lost for Man's creation,
All they smell is the fire's blaze,
Trees are slashed for the greater nation,
All they taste is each other's fear,
As the havoc rages on.

Matthew Hallett (11)
Ann Edwards Primary School, Cirencester

Bob's Life

I am a happy monkey called Bob.
The beautiful forest is my home,
With all my family and friends.
I am a happy monkey,
My favourite fruit is all around me,
Our world is wonderful and safe . . .

Early one morning there was a rumbling noise,
We all woke up with a fright.
Men with big axes and saws chopped down our homes.
Early one morning, all our food has gone!
So have the trees; we have no homes.
We are all feeling devastated and think we will die *soon!*

Early one morning good people came
With food, water and shelter.
'We are here to rescue you,' they said.
I am a happy monkey in a safe zoo
With my family and friends
In a nice enclosure forever!

Grace Bailey (10)
Bailey's Court Primary School, Bristol

Place Of Dreams

R is for rainforest, full of tall trees and exotic plants,
waterfalls so beautiful, shimmering in the sunshine.
A is for the animals that live in the forest, up in the trees,
down in the waters below, or wandering in the wonderful
greenery surrounding them.
I is for insects crawling and buzzing, keeping the food chain
going because that's what it needs.
N is for nature which the rainforest feeds; the beauty, the wonder,
which our future depends on.
F is for fearful animals as their homes are no more; habitats destroyed,
nowhere else to go.
O is for open spaces where trees used to sit, the wide open sky
looks down from above.
R is for rain which keeps the forests moist, warm climates,
dew on the leaves, birds singing in the distance.
E is for exotic, the word to describe this place; the colours,
plants and scenery can take your breath away.
S is for shimmering waterfalls gliding down the rock face,
listen to the thunderous noise and calmness that it makes.
T is for time to act and to show how much we care,
no more falling of trees, no more destroying beautiful things,
No more! No more!

Courtnie Williams (10)
Bailey's Court Primary School, Bristol

Recycle

Recycle things, don't throw them away
and they can be used another day.
For the world to be saved,
we must change how we behave.
So remember if it's glass, cardboard,
paper, plastic or tin,
recycle it, don't put it in the bin.

Zoe Wright (8)
Bailey's Court Primary School, Bristol

Echo Of A Tiger

There's a price on his head
He'll soon be dead
The hunter stalks his prey
There's a smile on his face today.

A mother plays with her cub
She shows him all her love
The pride happy but unaware
There's danger coming in the air.

One shot is all it takes
The cub looks on and shakes
His mother is now gone
How will he survive?
How will he carry on?

They take delivery of their new rug
Now's not the time to shrug
The stripes are on the floor
No longer a tiger's roar.

Not much longer now, tigers no more to see
Not much longer now
Tigers will be history!

Krista Matthews (10)
Bailey's Court Primary School, Bristol

I Put It In The Bin

I had a can of Coke, I put it in the bin!
I had a can of lemonade, I put it in the bin!
I had a can of juice, I put it in the bin!
I had a can of milk, I put it in the bin!
I had a can of squash, I put it in the bin!

What kind of bin?
The recycling bin!

Jade Fisher (8)
Bailey's Court Primary School, Bristol

Disasters!

They cut down the trees
They pollute the air
They throw litter on the ground
When the bins are just there
Just why are they doing this?
Do they just not care?
Do they not understand
Or do they think it's not fair?

Some people are wealthy
Some people are poor
Some people are hungry
Some people want more
Some people travel miles
Some people relax
Some people need help
Some people pay tax

But if someone can help
They'll be grateful enough
To cry tears of happiness
And make their eyes fill up!

Joshua Guy (10)
Bailey's Court Primary School, Bristol

Litter

Reuse, reduce, recycle are the stars,
So help the world, use the three Rs,
I don't think littering should be done,
Otherwise living on Earth won't be much fun.

Animals and litter just won't mix,
This is something we must fix,
Don't leave your litter on the ground,
Pick it up! Don't stand around.

James Hughes (10)
Bailey's Court Primary School, Bristol

Changes

Ever since my birth
I've lived on planet Earth
I opened my eyes
And to my surprise
The trees were green
The ocean was blue
And everything looked very new.

I am now eight years old
Sometimes I go out and it's very cold
In other places, it's very hot
This makes me sad because I am not
I watch the telly and to my surprise
The icebergs are melting before my eyes.

Human beings are to blame
Because none of us think the same
We should make a change before it's too late
All of us should contemplate
Let's get together and save Planet Earth
For our sons and daughters at their birth.

Lewis Scot Hedges (8)
Bailey's Court Primary School, Bristol

A Better World

We need to make the world clean and safe
So let us all work together
To make our future brighter
Let us do all we can
By each being a responsible child, woman or man

Keep your environment nice and clean
Stop dropping litter on the ground
Find a rubbish bin
To put your litter in.

Varun Thapa (9)
Bailey's Court Primary School, Bristol

About The Planet

Weather:

I feel sad because the weather is always bad.
We seem to have lots or rain.
I wish the sun would shine again.

War:
In war, people shoot each other with a gun.
I don't think this is much fun.
Instead of fighting each other,
Why don't they be nice to one another?

Pollution:
Near me there's a little stream
That is no longer clean.
Some people just don't care.
There are no fishes there.

Rainforest:
I am crying, because animals are dying.
Their homes and trees are being destroyed,
And this makes me annoyed.

Chelsea Reed (7)
Bailey's Court Primary School, Bristol

Going, Going, Gone!

Animals are just like money, going, going, gone.
Whales, tigers and many more, going, going, gone.
Trees being cut down, going, going, gone.
Being cruel to innocent creatures, going, going, gone.
Tigers shot for their fur, going, going, gone.
Turtles killed for their shells, going, going, gone.
Being greedy, taking too much, going, going, gone.
Murdering God's creation, going, going, gone.

Animals watching tourists being truly terrible beyond measure!

Sarah Hickman (9)
Bailey's Court Primary School, Bristol

The Giant Panda

Please save us

We are an endangered species
With less than a thousand of us
Left in the world

Please save us

We only live in bamboo forests in China
Where there are lots of lovely places to hide

Please save us

Stop taking our forests away
To build your homes and farms
We need them to run free and find food

Please save us

Stop killing us for our coats
After all we look better in them than you do!

Please save us.

Sophie Harper (10)
Bailey's Court Primary School, Bristol

Polar Bears

P ollution is killing me
O riginal home, the Arctic
L argest meat-eater on Earth
A dult polar bears live alone
R aw meat is what I eat

B igger than people
E at seals and fish
A rctic - save it
R oaming the ice
S ave the polar bears!

Katie Harper (7)
Bailey's Court Primary School, Bristol

Tidy Up!

Debris, debris, everywhere,
No one around to help or care.

Men go fishing for our tea,
Broken nets they let free.
A humpback whale or a turtle
Trapped for eternity.

Oil spilt in the ocean,
Penguins and seabirds left with no motion.

Families picnic on the sand
And leave behind all they do not want,
Plastic bottles, bags, Coke cans, chocolate wrappers
And cigarettes, all are bad.
Now a dolphin plays with a bag, now see it dead!
Now a human, glum and sad.

Tidy up and put away,
Then sea life can live another day!

Millie Thwaites (10)
Bailey's Court Primary School, Bristol

Endangered Animals - Let's Save Them

We love turtles so stop killing them
and turning their shells into guitars.
I like the slimy, slithering snakes so stop killing them
and turning their soft leathery skin into shoes, handbags and purses.
We love the cute, cuddly lions so do not turn them into
rugs, carpets and coats.
Stop cutting down the bamboo because pandas need to eat
bamboo to survive.

We all have the right to live in this world
so let's leave them
Alone!

Matthew Holgate (10)
Bailey's Court Primary School, Bristol

The Rainforest

Imagine the rainforest.
As the sun rises, the rainforest slowly wakes up,
the shining sun streams through the tops of the tall trees,
holding its green juicy leaves.
All the animals are waking up; monkeys screeching, bugs scuttling, jaguars stretching their long, tender paws out.
The beautiful rainforest is coming to life.
Now imagine what it would be like with no rainforest,
the animals are trying to survive but are slowly passing away,
what have we turned our rainforest into?
The trees that used to stand there giving us more oxygen,
they were our friends.
All the cute and cuddly animals that make you go, '*Aah,* how sweet'
are now becoming extinct.
What happened to the lovely tropical sound?
Now all I can hear are engines.
Help save our world!

Hattie Collins (10)
Bailey's Court Primary School, Bristol

Animals And Plants

Stop killing rare animals
Even if it is for money
Because they are lovely
And bees make honey
Lots of fish live in the sea
But Man fishes for too many
And if this keeps going on
Soon there won't be any
Don't drive, walk instead
Because flowers and plants will die
And if we kill all the plants and animals
It will make me cry.

Abigail Mathias (7)
Bailey's Court Primary School, Bristol

Animals Of Extinction

I look around and realise,
Most of the animals are gone,
Never again will one see that animal again.
A lot caused by the selfish ones,
Too lazy to walk.
Quite a bit caused for paper,
Cutting and destroying homes,
Maybe even melting them!
I see images in my head,
Not nice ones, no, but blue ones, heartbroken ones,
A polar bear waving its paw,
As its iceberg starts to sink.
Orang-utans looking down at me,
Their sadness shining through their faces,
I feel for them as the tree falls down.
I hope this will show the selfish ones what they're doing.
But I guess we can't change everyone.

Anya Clayton (10)
Bailey's Court Primary School, Bristol

Litter, Litter

Litter, litter, everywhere,
Wouldn't it be nice
If the streets were bare?
No one uses bins,
What's the point of them being there?
Don't you throw crisps on the floor,
Don't you throw down litter
When you're near your door,
When you're on a picnic,
Don't let it blow away,
Don't throw litter any day!
Use me!

Ruby Johnston-Stuart (8)
Bailey's Court Primary School, Bristol

Life As A Tree In A Rainforest

I
love
my leaves
and branches
because they are so
eye-catching. The view up
here is so spectacular. Monkeys
climbing through us trees. Birds fly
in-between our branches, then fly away.
The wildlife is so colourful. Crocodiles splash
in the Amazon, having a wonderful time. You like
forests so stop cutting down the rainforests or else
There
Will be
None
Of us
Left!

Megan Hiseman (9)
Bailey's Court Primary School, Bristol

If Only

Why can't I be free? Cos I'm living in poverty.
Nowhere to go, nowhere to hide,
No one by my side.
Feeling helpless, feeling scared.
Total despair cos no one cares.
Where am I to go? Where am I to stay?
No places to work or even to play.
I'm just a child and not very old.
I'm tired and hungry and very, very cold.
Why can't we help?
Why can't we share?
Let's work together to show some care.

Nathan Simon Dunn (11)
Bailey's Court Primary School, Bristol

Come Down To The Rainforest

Come down to the rainforest and see the fruit bats
and the slimy snakes.
Come down to the rainforest and see the howling monkeys
and the colourful toucans.
Come down to the rainforest and see the beautiful waterfalls
and the flowing rivers.
Come down to the rainforest and see the poisonous frogs
and the leaping jaguar cats.
Come down to the rainforest and see the scaly lizards
and colossal spiders.
Come down to the rainforest and see the tiny hummingbird
and enormous trees.
Come down to the rainforest and see that bit over there,
that bit, it's all bare!
Men from all around have cut down the trees.
Don't let this continue please!

Jaimie Hampton (9)
Bailey's Court Primary School, Bristol

A Message For The Hunters

Save the animals, like tiger, panda and black bear,
We don't need their skins to wear.
Stop the killing just for money,
The children of our world don't think it's funny.

We all want to keep the animals and see them grow,
So stop killing the animals, that's what we want you to know.

The leopard and lion are our biggest cats,
We don't want to use their skins for mats.
The world won't be right without all of these,
So stop the killing, please, please, please.

We all want to keep the animals and see them grow,
So stop killing the animals, that's what we want *you* to know.

Lauren Hicks (7)
Bailey's Court Primary School, Bristol

Endangered

Amazing and wonderful,
Every creature is precious;
Every time we change the environment,
For our own use,
By cutting down the forest,
We take out the animals' homes,
When poached for meat or fur, horns or tusks,
Our extraordinary creatures risk becoming extinct.
Some species only have about 50 of that kind,
But how can we save them?
By protecting all the animals' habitats,
And punishing those who hurt or kill them,
We can save the animals
From dying out
And never coming back to this Earth,
Wouldn't you be sad if the animals died out?

Sophie Williams (10)
Bailey's Court Primary School, Bristol

The Rainforest

The rainforest is a magical place.
When you are in it you cannot help but smile
and your smile will beam from ear to ear.
You can hear all the life that lives within and how beautiful it is!
Like the slithering of the snake,
the chattering sound of the monkeys
and the chirping of the birds,
mixing together to make the music of the forest.
It's a very green and wonderful place,
with the beauty of the trees and animals that live deep in the heart
of the rainforest.
We don't want to lose this magic,
So we need to work together to help it survive.

Holly MacDonald (10)
Bailey's Court Primary School, Bristol

Johnny Green

Oh Johnny Green, what should I do
To be eco-friendly just like you?
Oh Johnny Green, what should I do
To be eco-friendly just like you?

Walk to school or use the car pool,
Save our planet, no chemicals.

Oh Johnny Green, what should I do
To be eco-friendly just like you?
Oh Johnny Green, what should I do
To be eco-friendly just like you?

Energy-saving is the way,
This we should do every day.

Recycle your rubbish and turn off the lights,
So we can all be safe and sleep at night.

William Dennis (7)
Bailey's Court Primary School, Bristol

Sort It

Sometimes I feel very mad
When people are really bad
By not recycling a thing
Before they put it in the bin.

Paper, bottles, cans and foil
Cardboard, jars and old oil
To sort the rubbish they have got
It would really help a lot.

Just sort it out
It won't take long
Because if you don't
You know it's wrong.

Shay Norris (7)
Bailey's Court Primary School, Bristol

The Hunted Tiger

Here I crouch,
The hunted hunter.
My orange and black camouflage hiding me from the guns.
I see the wide-eyed men, the deadly guns, the great iron cage.
I pad behind the men, muscles tensing.
Suddenly I strike, charging at them, scattering them, clawing them.
A *click* draws my attention and I bound away before the bullets reach me.
Men chasing, then shooting, men yelling, 'Kill him!'
The trees start to claw me and I think,
I will end up as a dead dodo, following the fate of the poor passenger pigeon or the Stellar's sea cow.
Finally I see my fate,
A pellet strikes me, I see or move no more,
Death!

James Zhang (10)
Bailey's Court Primary School, Bristol

Meeting An Elephant In A Rainforest

One day I went to a rainforest,
I saw an elephant,
He came right up to me,
He looked angry.

I felt very scared,
I ask him why he was angry.
'Why are people cutting down my home?'
That's why he looked angry.

'We are sorry
We can help you.
We will plant more trees and cut down less.'
He looks happy now.

Ryan John Jackson (9)
Bailey's Court Primary School, Bristol

Animal Extinction

Goodbye to polar bears, goodbye to tigers.
Your extinction is drawing near.
If we don't help very soon,
One thing will be very clear.

You will be trapped behind glass doors,
For everyone to see.
Your fantastic roar and fabulous fur,
Will be a distant memory.

So if we stop pollution,
We will stop this situation,
From getting horribly worse.
So turn out the lights,
Walk to school,
At the end of this verse.

Molly May Westfield-James (10)
Bailey's Court Primary School, Bristol

Rainforest, Rainforest

Save the rainforest
Save the trees
Save the monkeys
Save us

Protect the rainforest
Protect the trees
Protect the monkeys
Protect us

Help the rainforest
Help the trees
Help the monkeys
Help us!

Adam Terry (7)
Bailey's Court Primary School, Bristol

Rainforests

Look in the rainforest, what do you see?
You see,
Poisonous frogs, scaly lizards and fruit bats,
Howling monkeys, snakes and shy jaguar cats.

You also see,
Trees praying with their branches.

You also hear,
Calling, falling, hearing, fearing, scaring, tearing, eating, beating,
Not to forget the unfortunate clashes and bashes
As the trees fall to their death.
We must help but how?
We must look after our world right now!

Lloyd Brown (10)
Bailey's Court Primary School, Bristol

When I See War On TV

I see little children crying,
Soldiers dead and people dying,
Tanks with holes in the side,
Homeless people trying to hide,
It makes me feel sad,
War is so bad.

Why do people fight?
Why can't they talk and be polite?
Not take things with guns,
Not argue, shout or run.
To make the world more fair,
We must learn to care and share.

Ieuan Boucher (8)
Bailey's Court Primary School, Bristol

Rainforests

R ainforests around the world are being cut down,
A nd no one is trying to save them,
I n rainforests lots of people live,
N ever will they move to a different habitat,
F rom the colossal Madagascar,
O r the tropical Amazon,
R ainforests are becoming destroyed,
E very day, big chunks of them are being cut down,
S omeone needs to act *now!*
T hough for some rainforests it's too late,
S omething needs to change to save the rainforests.

Rahul Dewan (9)
Bailey's Court Primary School, Bristol

Rainforests

R ainforests
A re being cut down,
I f we cut them down, animals will be endangered,
N ature is not the same,
F or us it doesn't look good,
O ver and over again, we get warned,
R eally we don't listen though,
E very day there is less wildlife,
S o,
T oday I give the warning,
S top cutting down trees!

Rebecca Nash (8)
Bailey's Court Primary School, Bristol

Polar Bears!

P olar bears are dying,
O n the ice they live.
L and is almost going,
A ll of us should help.
R educe, reuse, recycle,

B efore it gets too late.
E rase what you have done,
A nd change your way of life.
R espect the world we live in.
S ave polar bears today.

Annie Guy (7)
Bailey's Court Primary School, Bristol

Hunter Of The Ice World

P aws pad silently across the ice,
O ver the white blanket he proudly hunts,
L ooking for his prey is becoming a challenge,
A ll around him, the ice is melting,
R unning out of time, he's the last of his kind.

B efore manmade gases melt his home,
E veryone stop and think!
A re you a turned-off light? Or a computer on standby?
R educe CO_2 and,
S ave our polar bears!

Lewis Morgan (10)
Bailey's Court Primary School, Bristol

The Exotic Rainforest . . .

R educes carbon dioxide
A llows a place for animals to live and plants to grow
I nsects eat the plants there
N umbers of endangered animals live there
F ood for humans and animals
O ne of the rarest plants grows in rainforests
R ethink about destroying it
E very day medicines are found there
S top destroying the trees
T rees provide oxygen.

Jamie Dingley (10)
Bailey's Court Primary School, Bristol

Tiger Extinction

The magnificent tiger is playing in the forest prancing and running
as fast as he can.
The mean, cruel hunter kills all living things, *bang . . . bang . . .*
and the tiger is down.
The sad, sad tiger was killed this day for the selfishness of others,
for greed, of their fur.
Hundreds of tigers have been killed this way. This should stop
for the hope of their survival.
Stop, put the guns away
Too many tigers have been killed today!

Max Golder (10)
Bailey's Court Primary School, Bristol

Changing Our Ways

The world is here for all to see,
And it's a nice place for us to be,
If we all do our bit and help each other,
A better place it will be for another.
Aerosols, washing machines, too much heating,
The Earth does take a beating.
So if you want to make a difference,
Don't think you're being an interference,
Because if we don't try to change some things,
It won't be nice for future beings.

Joshua Adam Millard (10)
Bailey's Court Primary School, Bristol

Rainforest

Always Recycle
This will sAve our planet
Get Involved
Let's all plant New trees
To keep our Forests alive
Pick up Our rubbish
Rainforests are impoRtant
Be Eco-friendly
Always Switch off your lights
All of This will make a difference.

Leah Thompson (7)
Bailey's Court Primary School, Bristol

Tigers

Their soft, smooth, shining fur,
A striped tail as long as pasta,
Their big, watchful eyes,
And small noses.
Precious tigers that help complete the world.
We are all part of the circle of life,
And have the power not to break it.
It makes me feel sad.
It could be the end of tigers.
They are my favourite animals.

Annabel Best (10)
Bailey's Court Primary School, Bristol

Endangered Animals

E very animal needs our care.
N ow let's all help or some won't be there.
D odos are already extinct.
A ny animal could be next, which one do you think?
N ow you are all aware.
G o out and save the polar bear.
E lephants hunted for their tusks.
R hino horns are ground to dust.
E veryone can do their part.
D on't know how? Look in your heart!

Connor Boulton (7)
Bailey's Court Primary School, Bristol

If We All Could Be Green

If we all turn off the TV
When we are not watching it.
If we all turn off a light
When we don't need it.
If we all turn off the tap
When we brush our teeth.
And if we all use our world well
And keep our world clean,
This is what will make our world
Brighter and greener.

George Damsell (10)
Bailey's Court Primary School, Bristol

Recycling

Early one day, 'Is recycling good?' I asked my dad,
'But of course,' he said, 'recycling can never be bad.'
He said, 'Reduce, reuse, recycle soon,
Or the rubbish tip will reach the moon.
We must buy all the good and natural things,
No more disposable nappies or plastic rings,
If we recycle, we will be glad,
Because the Earth will be beautiful and not so bad.'
So I promise to recycle daily
And so do all the pupils of the Bailey's.

James Sparkes (7)
Bailey's Court Primary School, Bristol

Save The Planet

Help save the planet
Help save the planet
Please save the planet
Save the world because the animals' habitats
Are being cut down
And the rainforests are being cut down
And the Arctic and Antarctic are melting
Because of our cars
Use your car less
Please, help save the planet!

Emily Roebuck (7)
Bailey's Court Primary School, Bristol

Rainforests

R aining in the forest
A nimals all around
I n the depths of the rainforest
N ever cut trees down to the ground
F ruit for us to eat, they grow and give us
O xygen to breathe
R ecycle all your paper
E xtinction we don't need
S ave our precious rainforests
T oday!

Ciera Burns (8)
Bailey's Court Primary School, Bristol

The Day In The Amazon

R ain fell all day
A mazon rivers rose; as they flooded,
I slands formed
N ight fell
F orest grew noisy
O rang-utans slept soundly while
R odents scurried amongst the bushes
E agles swooped amongst the treetops
S ilence fell
T he rainforest was sleeping.

William Lopeman (8)
Bailey's Court Primary School, Bristol

Rainforest, Rainforest

Rainforest, rainforest
Please don't be sad
We're doing our best to save you
My mum's recycling
My dad's recycling
Even my brother's recycling
So rainforest, rainforest
Please don't be sad
Put on a happy face
And laugh out loud!

Liam Harvie (7)
Bailey's Court Primary School, Bristol

The Dreadful War

War is a bad thing so let's stop it all
and be friends.
We kill people in anger.
We are making people homeless and hungry.
Wouldn't you be depressed and hurt
if you lost your home?
We are putting everything in danger,
even ourselves.
Some people aren't as lucky as us
because we destroy everything they have.

Elisha Muscat (10)
Bailey's Court Primary School, Bristol

Stop Using Cars Now!

Stop using cars now
Or there will be loads of forest fires
And too much heat
And the Arctic will melt.
'We will die,' say the lemurs.
'We will drown,' say the lemurs
'Because the Earth will be nothing but water.'
So, turn off lights
When you're not in the room
And stop using cars now!

Matthew James Eastlake (7)
Bailey's Court Primary School, Bristol

Gas Environment

We don't take the car to school,
We always take the bicycle,
We realise that all that smoke,
Will make us choke,
So next time your mum says,
'Get in the car,' say to her,
'Do we have to! It's not that far!
We could walk or even bike it,
It's good for the environment
And you may even like it.'

Theodore Cox (7)
Bailey's Court Primary School, Bristol

Leave Our Rainforests Alone

R ainforest are natural wonders of the world.
A nimals in the forests are in danger.
I mpacts of global warming are huge.
N ot all parts of the rainforests have been found.
F act not fiction.
O ur responsibility is to stop deforestation.
R emind the world to think alike.
E missions of greenhouse gases must be reduced.
S top cutting trees down.
T ropical beauty.

Lauren Feltham (8)
Bailey's Court Primary School, Bristol

My World

Animals are endangered, we all know that,
We have to look after those big, wild cats,
Tigers, lions and elephants too
Are all endangered because of what we do.
Forests are going,
Ice caps are melting,
We can all help this with a bit of recycling.
What we do at home, at school and in the car,
Will help our world and our animals by far.

Heidi Sermulins (9)
Bailey's Court Primary School, Bristol

Our Survival

How do we make our planet a better place?
What does our world look like from outer space?
How can we let animals have a happy home?
How does a monkey feel when he is all alone?
What does a tree sound like when it is chopped to the ground?
Why do people leave rubbish lying around?
We need to save water, go on, give it a try
What would happen if all the water ran dry?
You will be asking, why?

Evie Bray
Bailey's Court Primary School, Bristol

Rubbish, Rubbish

R ubbish, rubbish everywhere
U nder bushes, in the fields and streets
B irds, hedgehogs, rabbits and mice all in danger
B ottles, cans, jars and tins must be recycled or animals will be trapped
I nside plastic bags, animals will climb, so tie a knot in them every time
S o clear away all your rubbish
H elp our animals to live long and be part of our world forever.

Danielle Fear (7)
Bailey's Court Primary School, Bristol

Recycling!

R ubbish is bad.
E co-kids to the rescue.
C are for your environment.
Y ou must help us to stop the pollution.
C ome on, let's save the world.
L ook around, what's happening?
I love my planet.
N ever give up.
G o, the big green poetry machine!

Eleanor Coyne (8)
Bailey's Court Primary School, Bristol

Former Jungle VIP

You may call me 'person of the jungle' or 'Jungle VIP',
But I am no longer safe high up in my tree.
Critically endangered. Forest reduced for cash.
Trees made into tomorrow's trash.
Is anyone listening?
Does anyone care?
Lend us an ear
Before we vanish,
Without anyone shedding a tear.

Kayne Richards-Bourne (10)
Bailey's Court Primary School, Bristol

How To Stop Pollution

P ollution is bad because it pollutes our atmosphere.
O ur world gets polluted because we don't look after it.
L itter pollutes our world if we drop it.
L et us save the Earth by recycling.
U se bikes instead of cars so much.
T o help the world, bring your own bags when you shop.
I can walk home instead of driving.
O il, is bad because it pollutes the sea.
N ow that's how we can stop pollution.

Samuel Grimwood (8)
Bailey's Court Primary School, Bristol

Recycling Is Good

R ecycling is good
E veryone should do it
C ome on everyone, have a go
Y ou can help the planet
C ans, paper, milk bottles and much more,
L ook at the labels carefully
I t is good to care
N o good just thinking,
G o and do it!

Lucy Ann Dunn (8)
Bailey's Court Primary School, Bristol

Being Homeless

I wander the streets, helpless and weak,
My stomach aches, the pain's so terrible,
I melt away into a corner,
People stare, their eyes pierce me,
The wind so sharp, it batters my cheeks,
I stare into windows in awe,
People are feasting on warm, plump chickens,
Painted with golden butter,
When I melt away into the cold.

Sara Millichamp (10)
Bailey's Court Primary School, Bristol

Don't Cut Down Trees

Hello!
I am a tree
Don't cut down me
My branches are tall but
You are small. My leaves are green
So don't be mean. I could be small or tall
And money does
Not
Grow on me.

Emilia Powell (8)
Bailey's Court Primary School, Bristol

Imagine

Imagine a winter with sunshine
Imagine a summer with snow
Imagine a spring with no leaves on the trees
Oh where did the seasons go?

We need to look after our world
So walk, don't drive
Turn off lights when not using them
To help keep our world alive.

Abigail Criddle (7)
Bailey's Court Primary School, Bristol

Litter Everywhere

Litter, litter everywhere, be sure to take care.
Put your litter in the bin, it's what to do if you want to win.
When you're walking down the street, you'll find litter at your feet,
Try to recycle as much as you can, just leave it out for the binman.
Don't drop litter anywhere, show other people that you care.

Ashley Hawtin (7)
Bailey's Court Primary School, Bristol

Being Homeless

I feel lucky and grateful to have a home
As it makes me sad to be alone.
I am upset because homeless people
have no money or food,
and they have to drink dirty water.
Some people can get very poorly,
they can get cold because they have no shelter.

I love my home and my family.

Georgia Hawkes (7)
Bailey's Court Primary School, Bristol

The Great Panda: The Bamboo-Eating Machine

Eating bamboo most of the day,
Maybe digesting some honey and bananas on the way.
Sitting around in their black and white coats,
Sometimes getting to captivity on boats.
Normally lives to at least twenty in captivity,
With the second longest tail in the bear family.

Lauren Sleight (9)
Bailey's Court Primary School, Bristol

Litter

L ots of sweets that use your cash,
I n the end it turns to trash.
T ry to clean up all your mess,
T he world will be a great success.
E ven if you feel bitter,
R emember to recycle litter.

Alfie Noott (9)
Bailey's Court Primary School, Bristol

Save The Planet

We all need to fight
The amount of light
So let's get involved
It's worth more than gold
It's all of our homes
And all of our lives
The planet counts on us
So let's start tonight.

Sara Thompson (7)
Bailey's Court Primary School, Bristol

Animals That Are Endangered

D olphins swimming in the sea
O nly a few are left
L ittle by little they are dying
P lease stop fishing with nets
H elp them
I n the ocean, dolphins are swimming
N ow and forever
S o save them today not tomorrow.

Megan Davis (9)
Bailey's Court Primary School, Bristol

War

A war began in the almighty jungle of Asia.
Deadly tearing and ripping each other's hearts out.
It's so heartbreaking as the dreadful teardrops fall slowly like nothing before.
Think about people who get killed or petrified and alive.
Stop the deadly war.

Sophie Jade Farr (10)
Bailey's Court Primary School, Bristol

Help Rainforests

We are losing Earth's greatest treasures,
Just as we are beginning to appreciate their value.
We are losing 137 plants,
Animals and species every day.
Because of the loss of them
Each time a rainforest gets destroyed.
It's like burning a library.
Help save rainforests to be a better person.

Henna Mistry (10)
Bailey's Court Primary School, Bristol

The World Is Changing

The world is changing,
It's getting sick.
To stop this happening,
We must act quick.
Recycle, walk, don't take the car,
These little changes will go far.
Let's help our planet, each get stuck in,
Don't turn the world into a dusty bin!

James Wakefield (8)
Bailey's Court Primary School, Bristol

Litter

L ittle pieces of rubbish left
I n the grass.
T ake me to my home, my home is
T he bin. I can either be an
E gg box or a drinks can, I am still
R ubbish.

Sam Cottle (8)
Bailey's Court Primary School, Bristol

Too Much

Too much litter on the street
We have got to keep it neat
Global warming everywhere
Pollution growing in the air
Not just the land but the sea too
Animals are dying because of you!
It's up to us to make a scene
We've got to keep our world green.

Kyle Prescott (9)
Bailey's Court Primary School, Bristol

It's Good To Recycle

It's good to recycle
Our bags, cans and bottles
Lots of energy to reuse
Good materials not to waste
If we all recycle
Our planet will be cleaner
Leaving clean air to breathe
For the kids of the future.

Emily Ford (9)
Bailey's Court Primary School, Bristol

Rainforest

I love monkeys,
They live in the rainforest.
People are cutting down trees
Poor funky monkeys
Where can they live and play?
Let's save the trees today.

Ollie Robertshaw (8)
Bailey's Court Primary School, Bristol

Save Our Seas

Litter scattered along the beach.
Tins and cans, bottles and bags.
Bags floating and bobbing on the surface of the water.
Cans and bottles twisting and turning.
We don't like rubbish in our gardens,
And neither do all the animals in the sea,
Like turtles, dolphins, whales and fish.
They don't get the chance to keep everything tidy.

Emily Louise Hammond (7)
Bailey's Court Primary School, Bristol

My World

In my world there are lots of people
More houses and traffic.
In my world the streets are not safe to play in.
In my world the cost of living has gone up so money doesn't go far.
In my world I have love and happiness.
This costs nothing, just a great family that I love.
My world; make it a happy, safe place for us all to be in.
My world.

Conor Stagg (9)
Bailey's Court Primary School, Bristol

Recycle!

Recycle your rubbish and start today,
No more excuses and no more delays,
Paper, glass and plastic is what you can save,
To pave the way to a greener day,
So please remember, pollution is bad,
It won't make you happy but it will make you sad.

Emily Wheeler (8)
Bailey's Court Primary School, Bristol

Think Rainforest

Think of all the animals dying in the rainforest,
Think about the green trees with nothing left to give,
How can we help the rainforest?
How will you do it?
Think about recycling your paper and card,
Think about using less fuel, it isn't that hard,
The world is so precious to us,
So think now!

Jessica Mead (8)
Bailey's Court Primary School, Bristol

Recycle

R ecycle, reduce and reuse
E veryone can help the environment by recycling
C ans, cardboard and cartons can be recycled
Y ears ago no one helped
C ardboard can be recycled into different things like toilet rolls and books.
L earn about it to save the planet
E nvironment can be saved by everyone around the world.

Morgan Jones (10)
Bailey's Court Primary School, Bristol

Hungry Children Of The World

H ungry children all over the land,
U nable to eat because they haven't any food,
N ow they can if we give a hand,
G ive a little something,
R emember they are struggling,
Y ou can help them and give it all it takes.

Mitchell Cox (10)
Bailey's Court Primary School, Bristol

Recycling

R ecycle newspaper once you have used them.
E nvelopes, when you have used them, don't chuck them away,
you can use them again.
C huck away in recycling bags -
Y ou should put any leftovers in the sort-it bins.
C hucking bottles away from your house that you have used, is bad.
L eave bags in your car so you can use them at a supermarket.
E very day recycle a little bit or a lot to help the environment.

Lauren Collins (8)
Bailey's Court Primary School, Bristol

Suffocation Of Earth

Car exhaust
Blowing hard
Fumes galore
Atmosphere thickening
Heat trap
Light trap
Global warming.

Kieran Perrott (8)
Bailey's Court Primary School, Bristol

Rainforest

Many colours to be seen
And all the trees are lots of shades of green.
The harmless trees swaying in the wind
Think of all the paper you have binned.
Reuse and recycle should be on your mind
There aren't many rainforests left
So please be kind!

Gemma Toghill (10)
Bailey's Court Primary School, Bristol

Recycle To Save The World

R ecycle as much as you can.
E verybody should recycle, even if you're a man!
C hildren will recycle so you can do it too.
Y ou recycle then do whatever you want to do.
C hildren learn to recycle to make the world a better place.
L et yourself recycle then tie up your lace.
E njoy recycling and have a piece of cake.

Caitlin Lee (8)
Bailey's Court Primary School, Bristol

Tiger, Tiger

Tiger, tiger, where are you tiger?
You used to run, hunt, leap and bound
as free as a bird but no more.
The hunters have come with their murderous polluting guns,
killing you and our environment,
and now we wear your beautifully-coloured fur.
What a very sad and self-destructing world we are living in.

Josh Doidge (11)
Bailey's Court Primary School, Bristol

Litter

Litter, litter leads to extinction
Litter, litter makes global warming
We should use the three Rs
We should take it out of nature
Then we can destroy it
Then we can stop global warming
We can make a difference.

Kjetil Rhem (9)
Bailey's Court Primary School, Bristol

How Would You Feel?

How would you feel if you had no home?
How would you feel if you didn't have a warm home to go to at night?
How would you feel if you didn't have clean water to drink?
Would you feel sad?
How would you feel if people were ill and there was no medicine?
How would you feel if you got no presents to celebrate Christmas?
Would you feel angry?

Ben Monks (10)
Bailey's Court Primary School, Bristol

Rainforest

Tall trees
Muddy water
Soggy mud
Long branches
Destroyed trees
Scary sounds
Green leaves.

Aaron Muscat (8)
Bailey's Court Primary School, Bristol

Save The Planet

Save the rainforest,
Save the trees,
Save the future of planet Earth please.
Keep the Earth green,
Keep the air clean.
This is our future,
This is our dream!

Jared Voisey (10)
Bailey's Court Primary School, Bristol

Cutting Down Trees

Cutting down the rainforest
Losing trees
We seem to do it with ease
But please
Don't cut down our trees
Save our planet
And help us breathe.

Cassidy Mae Bacon (8)
Bailey's Court Primary School, Bristol

Look After The World

R ecycle more paper, glass, cans, cardboard.
E veryone can do it!
C ars are bad for the environment!
Y ou and everyone can walk more!
C ycle to your local park.
L ive a happy life.
E veryone has got a job to do for the environment.

Carrie Quayle (7)
Bailey's Court Primary School, Bristol

Recycle World

Recycle world, start today
You don't even need to pay
Pick up your rubbish, don't throw it away
Put it in the recycle bin and start all over again
Tell everyone, spread the good news
That recycling has come to the world.

Hannah Carroll (8)
Bailey's Court Primary School, Bristol

Litter

L itter is bad
I t kills our universe
T o stop litter happening
T ry to stop littering
E co is much better
R ight from the start.

Grace Curnock (8)
Bailey's Court Primary School, Bristol

Save Our Rainforests

Think of all the animals dying everywhere,
Think of all the luscious trees with nothing to spare,
How can you help?
How will you do it?
If you don't take action, well shame on you,
So let's turn back time together and *stop!*

Georgia Collins (8)
Bailey's Court Primary School, Bristol

Saving The Planet

I feel happy when we turn lots of things off.
I feel sad when people waste more than they recycle.
I feel disappointed when I see cigarettes and chewing gum on the floor.
I feel shocked when I see a nuclear power plant.
The smell of smoke makes me feel full of carbon dioxide.

Kieran Klein (9)
Bailey's Court Primary School, Bristol

Racism

R acism must be stopped!
A ll around the world.
C hildren are judged by their skin colour.
I am going to change all that by learning other people's cultures.
S tand up for what you believe in!
M ake a difference - and learn about each other.

Melissa McCallum (8)
Bailey's Court Primary School, Bristol

Litter

L itter is a dangerous thing.
I t kills animals such as ducks and swans.
T ry to put your litter in the bin.
T o stop it, we need to work together.
E ach of us can play a part.
R educing litter can then start.

Sam Watkins (11)
Bailey's Court Primary School, Bristol

Animals In The Rainforest

Monkeys bounce from branch to branch
While colourful birds hop and dance.
On the forest floor down below
Mysterious creatures crawl and glow.
We need to stop cutting down trees
Because the animals ask us, 'Please!'

Enzo Steenkamp (8)
Bailey's Court Primary School, Bristol

Pollution

Don't go in the car if it's not too far.
Don't buy food that has travelled in an aircraft.
Don't switch on the lights if you don't need to.
Don't throw rubbish in the bin, recycle it.
Go on, make a difference if you dare
You can really change the world if you care.

Callum Wilson (8)
Bailey's Court Primary School, Bristol

The Rainforest

The sun shines down through the leaves,
Different shades of green combine together,
The gushing water races down the hill,
The vines twist in and out of the branches,
Animals adventuring through the forest,
Come back to a destroyed home.

Cole McKenzie (10)
Bailey's Court Primary School, Bristol

It Makes Me Feel . . .

It makes me feel . . .
Furious when people leave litter around.
Happy when people pick up their litter.
Awful when people don't pick up their dogs' poo.
Angry when people chuck their cigarettes out of their window.

Molly Cross (9)
Bailey's Court Primary School, Bristol

Save Our Planet

Recycle your rubbish,
Being eco-friendly is fun!
Use the right recycling bin,
Don't send it to landfill
And pollute our planet!

Megan Batty (8)
Bailey's Court Primary School, Bristol

Recycling

Dirty landfills puffing steam.
Trapping animals, spreading disease.
Make anew all of your old bits and bobs
And stinky things into bright new things.
Recycle and make me new!

Bethany Freeman (8)
Bailey's Court Primary School, Bristol

Recycling Is Good

Make sure that you recycle your glass,
So then we won't make greenhouse gas.

Recycle your paper and your cardboard,
And we will all live in a better world.

George Milewicz (7)
Bailey's Court Primary School, Bristol

Help Save The World

We can save the world by walking to school.
We can stop the pollution by making a rule.
Catch a bus or the train to stay out of the rain.
To help save the world.

Jack Furlong (7)
Bailey's Court Primary School, Bristol

I Feel . . .

Happy when I don't see dropped litter.
OK when I don't see people smoking.
Upset when I see cigarettes.
Disappointed when there is trash everywhere.

Bryony Constance (9)
Bailey's Court Primary School, Bristol

Helping The World

Helping the world is a great thing to do,
So if I can do it, then you can too.
If we do it together, it'll be so much fun
Helping the environment will be a good job done.

Lisa Millichamp (7)
Bailey's Court Primary School, Bristol

Green World

The world is a mess because rubbish is everywhere.
Save energy by using less electricity as it will be better
for the environment.
Animals need homes like people so save the rainforests.
Don't eradicate trees, for if they disappear we won't be able to breathe.
Car-share to cut down on fuel pollution.
It will work out well in the end only if we recycle.
It is a good thing so do it more.
Disease is a disaster so help make a cure to end world misery.

Together we can make the world
A brighter, better place.

Gregor Wright (10)
Barwick & Stoford CP School, Yeovil

Going Green

G oing green is the thing to do.
O nwards, upwards, go, be green.
I nternational crisis, what to do?
N o more litter dumped in holes.
G o on, recycle, make the world good.

G rab onto green initiatives, make the Earth cleaner.
R educe, reuse, recycle, rethink.
E conomy needs help from us all.
E veryone needs to play their part.
N ow we can start to save the Earth.

James Fay (11)
Barwick & Stoford CP School, Yeovil

Creatures

C is for chickens, we breed them for eggs.
R is for rabbits, you can keep them as loveable pets.
E is for elephants, they help with work in India.
A is for ants who, despite being tiny, play an important role on this Earth.
T is for trapping seals which must be stopped.
U is for umbrella birds.
R is for recycling, we can all play our part.
E is for environment, it's slowly dying.
S o do something to help and save our future - now!

Dan Thick (11)
Barwick & Stoford CP School, Yeovil

Animals Extinct

Can you help?
Because there is no leather
And no skinned coats.

Animals, animals,
How will they live?
They won't be able to eat or drink.

Sea turtles, sea turtles
How lovely you are
But if you die
You won't be as you were.

Animals, animals,
How will they live?
They won't be able to eat or drink.

Squirrel, squirrel
As brown as a tree
But if you are dead
We mustn't agree.

Tia Hannon & Jessica Davis (9)
Castle Batch Primary School, Weston-super-Mare

Recycling

You can help save
The environment more.
I think you should know
That animals are being
Harmed by the littering
A lot.

Please help,
Please help,
You can save the
Environment.
You can save the
Environment.

You can help by
Recycling more paper.
More and more animals
Are getting diseases.

Please help,
Please help,
Saving the environment
Is very hard work
So please help.

Lauren Maynard (9)
Castle Batch Primary School, Weston-super-Mare

Pollution

Pollution, pollution, it's our fault
Pollution, pollution, it's really us
Pollution, pollution, sunny days may be gone
Pollution, pollution, ice that melts
Pollution, pollution, rainforests cut down
That explains Earth's frown!

Lily Badger (10)
Castle Batch Primary School, Weston-super-Mare

Don't Be A Criminal

Turtles are dying
Why, oh why?
You may think it's fun
But it's killing hundreds
Of marine animals.

Tigers are dying
Oh why, oh why?
Because the poachers
Are out.

Fishermen fish
Dolphins die
Nets get trapped
Round their noses
What do you do?

Monkeys are dying
Including the chimpanzee
Upon your knee.

Elephants are dying
People want their tusks
Just to put on the wall!

Whale so big
Why do we kill you?
Just for shoe polish
And lipstick.

Polar bear, polar bear
White as snow
Electricity is killing you
Why, oh why?

There'll be no world
Without them
And that's your fault!

Rebecca Fletcher (9) & Miel Beck (10)
Castle Batch Primary School, Weston-super-Mare

Help The Underwater World

The sea is not a rubbish bin
Recycle it and all will live
And do your bit for the environment
Because the sea is not a litter bin.

Animals get injured
And animals die
All sea creatures
Will have to say goodbye.

Some people fish in the wrong places
And some turtles get injured faces
Jellyfishes' tentacles dangle all day
You don't want this to stop
So help us in any good way.

Animals get injured
And animals die
All sea creatures
Will have to say goodbye.

Please recycle
We don't want things to die
Please recycle
We don't want to say goodbye.

Animals get injured
And animals die
All sea creatures
Will have to say goodbye.

Amy Richardson & Lucy Veale (9)
Castle Batch Primary School, Weston-super-Mare

The Rainforest

Deep, deep down in the rainforest
Where the African people live
We cut down trees and they start to bleed
And we don't help them a bit.

When we cut down trees
You're hurting me
Because I need oxygen
And I don't help a bit.

Deep, deep down in the rainforest
Where the African people live
We cut down trees and they start to bleed
And we don't help them a bit.

The treetops grow
But you don't know
That it kills us and our world.

Deep, deep down in the rainforest
Where the African people live
We cut down trees and they start to bleed
And we don't help them a bit.

Bethany Maidment (9)
Castle Batch Primary School, Weston-super-Mare

Rainforest

Rainforest, rainforest, rainforest,
When you're cutting down trees
You're cutting down me
So you better stop now!

Rainforest, rainforest, rainforest,
We can't live without air,
Otherwise we will explode
And no one will survive.

Samantha Bryant (9)
Castle Batch Primary School, Weston-super-Mare

Let's Recycle

No time to waste,
It's up to you,
You can do it,
Don't get in a stew.

Recycle, recycle, recycle,
Let's travel
By bicycle,
Go green.

Let's recycle everything,
Like bottles, cans and jars,
So help us recycle please,
But remember, don't travel by cars!

No time to waste,
It's up to you,
You can do it,
Don't get in a stew!

Elizabeth Parker (9)
Castle Batch Primary School, Weston-super-Mare

The Rainforests

People are cutting down trees,
We need our trees to help us breathe,
I know that people need the wood,
But it's not doing any good.

Animals are losing their homes,
And all they can do is moan,
So if you carry on,
The monkeys will be gone.

So as you can see,
If we don't stop now,
None of us will be free.

Chloe Avonia Patterson (9)
Castle Batch Primary School, Weston-super-Mare

It's Our Planet: Earth

The world is crying
Dodos dying
And now all their species are gone.

We're chucking out litter
It's all becoming bitter
It's not being put where it should.

The water is dirty
Humans are becoming thirsty
We should have thought about it before.

It's all getting hotter
It's a bit of a bother
And where will the polar bears live?

The world is dying, what shall we do with me and you?
So save it, love it, look after it.
It's our planet: Earth.

Olivia Emily Elliott (9)
Castle Batch Primary School, Weston-super-Mare

The Animals Will Soon Be Gone

Animals will soon be gone,
Their habitats
Are being destroyed,
Soon there will be none,
Our world will be done.
Animals will soon be gone,
Camels can last for days and days,
But they can die in different ways.
Animals will soon be gone,
Soon there will be less and less,
For our world is turning into a big mess!

Alana Lindsay (9)
Castle Batch Primary School, Weston-super-Mare

The Environment

Ice caps being destroyed
Ocean levels rising
Penguins and polar bears dying
We need to do something
Hotter and hotter
The planet Earth
It's not much worth.

CO_2 in the atmosphere
Destroying the world
Without fear.
We need to recycle
We need to stop
We need to think
Before we're destroyed
Without a blink!

Steven Eveleigh (9)
Castle Batch Primary School, Weston-super-Mare

The Lost World

The lost world is suffering
Because climate change is here
Help it, save it, mankind can do it.

The sea has been polluted
In many different ways
It has been that way forever.

Animals are facing extinction
Many will be gone
The world is following on

Recycle, reuse and reduce
There is no excuse
Our Earth needs it, help it, save it!

Georgia Elizabeth Carpenter (9)
Castle Batch Primary School, Weston-super-Mare

Be Green

Ice caps melting in the sun
Global warming's just begun.
Animals dying in the sun
Global warming's just begun.
It all used to be so clean with hygiene
But now it's a polluted mushy green.

You should know what not to do
Don't flush things you shouldn't down the loo.
The oil clogs up the animals' lungs.
The global warming's just begun.

Global warming, the dying's begun
The animals are dying one by one.
Global warming's just begun.

Global warming's just begun!

Jade Masters (9)
Castle Batch Primary School, Weston-super-Mare

Stop The Litter, Keep The Trees

Stop the litter, keep the trees,
Be kind to the environment, you and me need.

Bin it, don't throw it,
Please recycle it, reuse it,
Stop annoying the animals,
Keep the litter to yourself,
You can do it if you respect everyone else.

Stop the litter, keep the trees,
Be kind to the environment, you and me need.

Stop polluting the world, don't travel by car,
Cycle to school,
Cycle to shops.

Chloe Brinn (9)
Castle Batch Primary School, Weston-super-Mare

Endangered Animals

Animals are dying, rainforests too
What are you going to do?
Look in the fields
Look in the forests
What are you going to do?

Flowers, towers, sun and shine
Sunny bunny, too young to die
Hotter, hotter, the planet grows
Dying, dying, not allowed
Being healthy keeps it clean
But it's not yet all extinct
But it soon will be.

Animals endangered
Just begun.

Amanda Prosser (9)
Castle Batch Primary School, Weston-super-Mare

Recycling

R educe, reuse, recycle.
E xtinction; animals like dodos are already extinct,
orang-utans and mountain gorillas could be next.
C limate change is affecting our weather,
which means less sun in the summer and less snow in the winter.
Y esterday we can put behind us but we can't put recycling
behind us because otherwise our world will be endangered.
C ardboard and paper can make a big difference if we recycle it.
L itter is being dropped all over the world.
I ce is melting.
N asty CO_2 is being turned into O_2 by trees.
but if we keep cutting them down, they won't be able to change it.
G lobal warming, we have already started!

Bethany Louise Kemmish (9)
Castle Batch Primary School, Weston-super-Mare

Rainforests

They're cutting down the rainforests!
Don't cut down trees!
We can do it, mankind can do it!
Just don't cut down trees!

You're killing the animals
Don't cut down trees!
We're doing it too
So don't cut down trees!

Help save the environment
Don't cut down trees!
Oxygen, it's good
Really, don't cut down trees!

Luke Russe
Castle Batch Primary School, Weston-super-Mare

Poacher's Prey

Surging through rainforests
Full of fear
From the poacher's eye
The picture of a white tiger
Prowling through the grass
As the tiger's feathery fur brushes on the long grass.

Suddenly a bird calmly flies over the tiger
The tiger catches the bird
The bird thrashes to escape the tiger's clutches
As the bullet hits the frightened tiger
The white tiger drops to the ground and weeps for mercy.

Now the white tiger is gone and forgotten.

Chloe Knight (9) & Ella Badger (10)
Castle Batch Primary School, Weston-super-Mare

The Lost Life

People crying, for the world is dying
Falling apart at the loss
Public places are all disgraces
The murky green rivers won't clean.

Lives are lost, say bye to the compost
Tears will fall, listen to it all
The nightmare, the nightmare,
It's come.

Animals were there,
But now we're crying in despair,
For all our places are gone
And the world is switched off!

Katie Louise Handley (9)
Castle Batch Primary School, Weston-super-Mare

Don't Cut Down The Rainforest

Don't cut down the rainforest
Because you're killing animals
And it's our fault.

People who cut down trees
They're killing the world!
If you cut down . . .
Plant more!

Help save the environment
People who cut down trees
Shouldn't because the oxygen is going away!

Thomas Starr (9)
Castle Batch Primary School, Weston-super-Mare

Save Animals' Habitats

Save the animals' habitats.
Save the animals' habitats.
If you don't they will all die
And there will be none left.

Don't hurt the animals' habitats.
Don't hurt the animals' habitats.
If you do, they will run away
And we won't see them again.

So let's not hurt the animals' habitats.
So let's not hurt the animals' habitats.
So if you see someone hurting the habitats
Tell them to stop!

Lauren Girling (8)
Longwell Green Primary School, Bristol

Butterflies

Let the butterflies pollinate,
Don't let them become extinct.
Don't cut the flowers down,
Just don't eat the butterflies
And just let the butterflies live.
I just love the butterflies flying in the air,
Just keep planting seeds so we can make more flowers.
I've seen so many lies
From people saying that they're not eating butterflies,
Don't build houses on the flowers.

Jamie Griffin (8)
Longwell Green Primary School, Bristol

Trees

Recycle your paper,
It saves us cutting down trees.
Trees are living things you know,
Soon there won't be any trees,
The trees will be paper.
So please take care of your paper,
We haven't got any seeds left.
Don't cut down trees
They're living things.

Millie Brown (8)
Longwell Green Primary School, Bristol

Butterfly Do This

Butterfly, butterfly
Please don't go.
Butterfly, butterfly
We want to know.
We don't want to hurt you,
We just want to watch you.
Come out butterfly,
Please don't go.

Maeve Crozier (8)
Longwell Green Primary School, Bristol

Butterfly, Butterfly

Butterfly, butterfly, fly to me,
Butterfly, butterfly glide to me,
Butterfly, butterfly dance to me,
Butterfly, butterfly fly all around,
Butterfly, butterfly don't touch the ground.

Olivia Davis (8)
Longwell Green Primary School, Bristol

Cycling And Recycling

Cycling and recycling do the job,
Don't drive,
We want to be alive.
Use bins, don't use the floor,
'Cause we are saving the world.
If you wanna save the Earth
Follow the tips and we'll all be fine.

Ben Harris (8)
Longwell Green Primary School, Bristol

Dive Dolphin

Dive dolphin, dive through the shiny sea,
Jumping through the waves very happily,
Catching all the fish as they swim by,
Jumping through the air, splashing through the sea,
Making big splashes as it swims by,
Now the day is over it's time to go to sleep,
Now it's getting tired, time to sleep.

Rebecca Masters (8)
Longwell Green Primary School, Bristol

Save The World

Butterflies twist, butterflies twirl,
Come on let's save the world.
Pretty patterns butterflies carry
Down in the deep, dark alley.
Trees are green, planet Earth is blue,
If you want to save the world it's up to you.

Ashleigh Hill (9)
Longwell Green Primary School, Bristol

Fly Butterfly, Fly

Fly butterfly, fly
Through the deep blue sky
And twinkle and glide
Through the glowing sun
Until the day is done
So fly butterfly, fly.

Abbey Schlick (8)
Longwell Green Primary School, Bristol

Butterfly, Butterfly

Butterfly, butterfly play with me.
Butterfly, butterfly can you see
That you are sitting on my knee?
Butterfly, butterfly bye bye,
Come again some other time.

George Honeywell (9)
Longwell Green Primary School, Bristol

Butterfly, Butterfly

Butterfly, butterfly please play with me
Butterfly, butterfly please eat my tea
Butterfly, butterfly sing with me
Butterfly, butterfly say goodbye to me.

Daniel Tancock
Longwell Green Primary School, Bristol

Sweet Butterfly

Butterfly, butterfly stay around
Butterfly, butterfly fly around
Butterfly, butterfly collect pollen
Butterfly, butterfly collect pollen more often.

Nathan Gregory (8)
Longwell Green Primary School, Bristol

Man Noticed Too Late

A man is alive,
He does not drive,
He grows his own food,
He's always in a good mood,
He's a nice man,
He tries not to get a tan,
He hates the sun
And pays a ton
For his rent,
I don't think he should pay that, he's meant
To look after us,
So why did the hunters make a fuss?
And kill all the animals badly,
Sadly,
He was not able to help though he tried,
And now the world has cried.
Why didn't we help and see?
The man is the help we need,
To succeed.

Emily Rose Derrick (9)
Luckwell Primary School, Bristol

Destroying Trees And Homes

Chop, chop, chopping,
Destroying homes.
Killing oxygen,
Not planting more.
Being cruel,
Not caring.
Think about themselves
Just for money.
Distressed animals
Dying of fright.
Basically murdering,
Does that make it right?
Making populations
Of forests small.
Now making the world
A bad place to be.
Well, who wants that?
Definitely not me!

Shannon Warren (10)
Luckwell Primary School, Bristol

The Simple Way

You only need to do one thing
so do it the simple way.
Walk, don't drive,
that's the simple way.
Switch off the lights,
that's the simple way.
Put things in the recycling bin,
that's the simple way.
So do it . . .
the simple way!

Ella May Thomson (10)
Luckwell Primary School, Bristol

Spread The Word

I am calling from every corner of the world,
The poor world which we have destroyed.
I am calling for someone to listen,
To listen to what I have to say:

There's only *one* way to save the world;
For *you* to make a difference.
Can *you* walk to school or work tomorrow?
Can *you* turn off the TV without leaving it on standby?

Now you have heard what I have to say.
Now think what you can do . . .
I mean what I have said
And I hope it doesn't sound like gibberish to you!
I'm saying this for a reason, a reason which I can do.

Spread the word!

Hannah Turner (10)
Luckwell Primary School, Bristol

Don't Use Cars

D on't use cars they are bad. Use cars
O nly if it is urgent. Say
N o to cars they waste oil, fuel and
T oo much money.

U se cars only if you live a long way from things,
S top using cars. they are ruining the world.
E very day people are doing their part to ruin the world.

C ars are bad. Stop using them please, they are terrible.
A re you wanting to ruin the environment?
R evving their engines, it is just annoying.
S tart to walk to places. Don't be lazy!

George Jonathan (10)
Luckwell Primary School, Bristol

The Big Green Machine

In the world there are bees,
To be eco-friendly you will need trees.

Landfill sites are bad,
It makes people sad.

Turn all lights off when you should,
Save electricity, it's good.

In your kitchen reuse tins,
Don't put them in your bins.

Help our world too,
Do things you should do!

Beth Price (10)
Luckwell Primary School, Bristol

Save The World

R eusing
E ach day
C an help a lot.
Y ou look and see what you've done.
C an you recycle each day?
L ove recycling, what about you?
I love it, what about you?
N ow I help you, we're
G oing to save the world.

Kelsey Victoria Shopland (9)
Luckwell Primary School, Bristol

On A Monday Morning

On a Monday morning when you go to school
You jump in the car like a lazy fool.
You put the key in and the engine turns on
And you say goodbye to your dear dad John.
You're wasting your money on petrol too,
But then you decide to walk, you're not spreading pollution,
Well done to you.
Try to walk to school,
It will be *cool!*

Ellie-Marie Eyres (11)
Luckwell Primary School, Bristol

The Big Green Machine

R ecycling is one thing
E veryone can do
C ompost is good for our community
Y ou can help us too!
C aring for our planet means
L itter goes in the bin
E verything to be treated with 100%.

Please help us with the big green machine!

Francesca Belgium (10)
Luckwell Primary School, Bristol

It's The End Of The World!

When drugs are gone, they're gone,
When the lights are blown out, they're gone,
When the trees rot, they're gone,
And when the last thing on Earth's gone
We're doomed!

Shayla-Millena Jackson (10)
Luckwell Primary School, Bristol

Please Do The Small Things That Help Us!

You only have to do small things,
When my mum does them she sings.
She turns off the light
When she's going to bed at night.
Instead of taking the car
You can walk quite far.
Please do these small things
And you'll be like queens and kings.

Lani Cooke (11)
Luckwell Primary School, Bristol

Recycling

There was an old man from Ashton
He recycled every day,
He recycled cans and bottles,
He recycled tins in bins.
So that old man in Ashton,
Just think about him now
When you're about to chuck away a tin or a can
Stop, think, recycle, help the world.

Olivia Meacham (10)
Luckwell Primary School, Bristol

Eco-Kid

E nergy-saving
C ompost maker
O nly drives battery cars

K eeping healthy
I nvolved with charities
D igging holes for plants.

Leah Ivanov (10)
Luckwell Primary School, Bristol

Recycling

Bugs, worms, beetles, food,
Sounds like a job for Green Machine.
Remember the three Rs; reduce, reuse and recycle.
Save animals,
Save the environment,
Dustbin says, 'Feed me now!'
Just turn your back and say,
'No! Not now!'

Aimée Stanfield (10)
Luckwell Primary School, Bristol

Recycle Rap

All the things that you use,
Don't put them in the bin.
Cartons, paper, plastic, metal and lots and lots of tins.
If you recycle you will be a gold star.
If you keep recycling you'll go very far!
Now you can do it, you are a star.
Always recycle and walk, don't use the car.

Lily Iles (10)
Luckwell Primary School, Bristol

Rubbish, Rubbish, Rubbish!

Rubbish, rubbish everywhere,
Rubbish, rubbish we don't care.
Down the corridors and up the street,
This is where the rubbish meets.
Now down the river and the stream
All our rubbish is just plain mean.

Ruby Gregory (9)
Luckwell Primary School, Bristol

Importance For The World

To recycle is very hard,
Green and brown and white.
These are all the colours of the bottles
And the important truck,
With a honk here, a honk, honk there.
Green and brown and white.

Aaron Sandy (10)
Luckwell Primary School, Bristol

Stop The War

War is nasty, a lot of people die.
Why do people die?
It should be the war that dies.
So have peace in the land
And stop the war - it's really poor.

Chad Scragg (10)
Luckwell Primary School, Bristol

Pollution

We all know it's bad
So don't even think about it.
Why don't we do anything about it?
Why do we pollute?
That question puzzles me so much.

Jasmin Taylor (10)
Luckwell Primary School, Bristol

Keep Us Alive

Recycling is very important because it will save the planet.
Compost will save the planet.
Turn out the lights when you leave a room.
Stop cutting trees down because trees give us oxygen
And keep us alive.

Tom Woodburn (10)
Luckwell Primary School, Bristol

Why, Oh Why?

All the trees help us live,
So why, oh why do people chop trees down?
It is heartbreaking for animals
So why, oh why do people chop trees down?

Daniel Farr (10)
Luckwell Primary School, Bristol

World Peace

Make our world a better place,
Wars and fighting, a disgrace,
Put all guns and bombs down,
Or give all creatures a massive frown.

Ryan Keith Kent (9)
Luckwell Primary School, Bristol

To Money Cravers

Only when the last gun has been shot,
The last tree has been cut
And the last endangered animal eaten,
Will we realise we can't eat money.

Rhiannon Lucy Lewis (9)
Luckwell Primary School, Bristol

Stop!

Stop the drugs, they ain't gonna work!
Get rid of drugs!
Never smoke or you'll turn into a bug!

Jack Farr (9)
Luckwell Primary School, Bristol

Our World

Save our world for good
Make our world a better place
And you'll feel it too!

Jack Gregory (10)
Luckwell Primary School, Bristol

Our World

Stop cutting trees down
Everywhere will be a town
We have harmed our Earth.

Rachel Cheung (9)
Luckwell Primary School, Bristol

The Three Rs

Reduce, reuse, recycle
We can save the world
With these three special words.

Gabriel Dekany (9)
Luckwell Primary School, Bristol

A Loveable Beast

A loveable beast,
Preparing itself to pounce on its defenceless prey.
The creature bounds forward,
And snatches the young fawn from its mother's side.
The animal suffocates the fawn and
Eats slowly, enjoying every bite,
Blood around his lips.
This gorgeous creature is being destroyed,
As white as snow and as black as coal,
Help the beast survive.
The animal is . . .
A tiger.

Ferocious tiger,
Roaring lion,
Charging rhino,
Stomping elephant,
Creatures wanting survival.
Hunters with their guns and bombs,
Are too greedy and couldn't careless.
The poachers need to be taught a lesson,
Need to be destroyed.
Protect all the animals.

Freya Holmans-Price (10)
Milverton CP School, Taunton

Rainforest

An admirable, imaginative, chattering atmosphere,
The enjoyable, entertaining, remarkable survivors,
Whose habitats have been destroyed.
Deforestation is biting an almighty chunk
From animals and their habitats.

Despairing
Miserable,
Years of wood cutting,
The unfortunate animals sit and watch
Their fabulous habitats being wasted.

The trees stand proud on a floor of soggy leaves,
Small animals scuttling beneath its beautiful, colourful trunk.
When morning comes the rainforest awakes!
The animals start their exciting day.
Whilst a sky of green leaves dance and sway in the breezy wind
By cutting down trees you are destroying a wonderful habitat!

Matilda Blundell (10)
Milverton CP School, Taunton

Black Smoke

The gloomy smoke hung in the sky like a stalking animal,
Its raven walls stand tall and keep the grim mystery inside,
The fumes oozing out of its mouth in murky bunches of polluted air.

Pollution is a colossal black hole sucking in the planet it discovers,
Our world is like a hot air balloon about to burst,
Sustainable energy,
Graceful wind turbines,
Gleaming solar panels,
If we carry on like this,
What will happen to us?
We don't know . . .
Do you?

Lucy Ayres (10)
Milverton CP School, Taunton

Polluting The World

Rubbish piled high nearly reaching the sky
It makes me feel sad, guilty, unhappy and bad.
Bulldozers squashing the rubbish down
But still growing higher
Wildlife is found but most homeless.

Please help our planet Earth
And all the other animals
Otherwise they might die
All the crops will get killed or drowned
And that will leave us with nothing.

Ice caps are melting
Polar bears will starve
So fish won't swim under the ice so willingly
The mud might harm the polar bears and all the other animals
The really sad thing is that it is mostly our fault
And the only thing we can do is help to put things right.

Anna Kennedy (8)
Milverton CP School, Taunton

Deforestation

A hideous smudge on the landscape
A revolting monster soaking up the turquoise trees
And creating an almighty bruise on the terrain.

Trees need to be replaced, we need to sustain the planet,
Renew the rainforests.
The forests have been shattered into shards of khaki woodland
Disgraceful people determined to crush what's left.
Look at the future, the trees have gone.
Humans have demolished them.
We must fix it for other generations
Only we can stop it happening.

Oliver Eyres (11)
Milverton CP School, Taunton

Extinction

A beautiful fantastic bird
roaming the land as the plants whistle by its side.

Poached to extinction
by the evil that destroys this planet.

This awfulness has to stop.
How many more amazing creatures will it take?

To stop this happening,
we need to educate people about disastrous torture.

As well as protecting all of our safari parks
from the terrible poachers who kill these fantastic creatures.

If we can stop this happening,
we will be on our way to saving this planet.

We can save the world,
but everyone will have to do their little bit.

Will Maunder (10)
Milverton CP School, Taunton

The Destroyer

Turned up earth, as red as fire.
Crashing trees falling to the ground,
Chainsaws revving like raging bears,
Killing nature's habitat, destroying their homes.
Loaded trucks, overflowing with logs,
Destroying the earth as they work.
Burning fumes as they continue destroying the forest.

Thudding trees smashing up the Earth,
Wheels spinning, trucks stuck in the red clay.
Skylines turning petrol, spinning cranes picking up the logs.
Nothing left from the landscape apart from turned up earth.

Aaron Baker (11)
Milverton CP School, Taunton

Poisonous Gases

We are
wasting resources,
choking horses.
This is bad,
I feel so sad.
Stop, this is bad,
it makes me mad.
They are mean,
they should be green.
They are making gases
that are destroying our world,
polluting our world
and choking our world.
We must stop this
before it is too late.

Jeremy Pearson (9)
Milverton CP School, Taunton

Extinction

An animal of extreme elegance and gifted powers waiting to explode,
This animal has heartbreaking, depressing, suffering, tearful memories that have to go.
The king of the jungle,
The proud and powerful beast is being extinguished,
Halt the hunters,
Protect the animals, stop extinction.

When the proud and beastly animals are gone, you will regret what you have done.

Stop extinction, stop now.

Melissa Tucker (10)
Milverton CP School, Taunton

The Future Of The Forest

Rampaging streams begging for mercy,
Animals need more habitats
That's what they deserve
Don't upset the beautiful fresh jungle
The jungle faces a sharp blade
The pretty plants that live together
That have the same roots but different in their feelings.

Recycle!
That's all you need
Trees deserve to live
Just let them be
Let the chain rust
Trees control time
Let them decide the future.

Emily Lee (10)
Milverton CP School, Taunton

Eco World

Factories polluting the world.
Can't see green world.
Polar bears scavenging for food.
People must be green.
It's shocking, climate changing.
CO_2, ban it.
Put paper in the recycle bin.
Keep wildlife, it's lovely.
Be eco for our world.
It will be a better world.

George Bolton (8)
Milverton CP School, Taunton

Make Earth Clean

Pick up your litter, put in the bin
Don't leave it lying around
Recycle it
Recycle it
Recycle it
Litter is bitter and it's red, blue and white
Green, silver
Gold and black
Make Earth clean.

Josh Tickner (9)
Milverton CP School, Taunton

The Pollution Disaster

A city, is big, annoying and spoils the world.
The temperature is warming up so the Earth is cracking up.
Some people are homeless because their homes
have been knocked down.
Places have been flooded because people are polluting the world.
It's creating warmth, melting the ice caps, letting more water
into the sea and overflowing the land.
Trees are being cut down for furniture.
Factories have a big grey cloud above them.

William Tuaima (8)
Milverton CP School, Taunton

Peace

What I want for the world is peace,
Stop people being poor and suffering.
Be cheerful and think how much luckier
You are than some others.

I hate to see animals die
From pollution which leaks and kills.
I'm thankful of those who give time to help.

Let's stop the pollution that kills the world.

Rosie Stanton (9)
Milverton CP School, Taunton

Extinction Of The Dodo

Extinction is a dump with every animal drowning in a pit!
The hunters rampaging like a tornado, hauling up the animals
Protection for creatures
Before the hunters demolish the planet!

Extinction is a coal-black, murky oil
Murdering every creature that discovers the glaring eye!
You might ask who is the lurking mysterious shadow!
. . . You

Olivia Anne Hooper (10)
Milverton CP School, Taunton

Pollution Poetry

Elephants, tigers, every animal - save them all
Don't cut down rainforests
- Leave them standing tall
When you wake in the morning
It's lovely to hear birds singing
With joyful cheer
Leave the world alone, leave it in peace
It's time for pollution to cease.

Toby Eyres (9)
Milverton CP School, Taunton

Pollution Poem

Now pollution is bad
and makes me sad.
Our world is in gloom
so let's make some cleaner room.
Now I'm ashamed,
let's make our world good again.
Being eco is a good thing to do
to make the world better for me and you.

Connor Cutler (9)
Milverton CP School, Taunton

Eco World Warrior

Polar bears forage on dry ground trying to hunt for food
Brown muddy water flooding towns and cities
Oil factories filling the air with pollution and greenhouse gases
Black dry drought that is made from having no rain
Smog clouds hovering over large cities and continents
Bulky holes squealing with pain.

Emily Stewart (8)
Milverton CP School, Taunton

A Poem To Help The World

More than 1,000 birds die because of the pollution within the sea,
It's very shameful and hurtful to me,
Al those dirty colours - black, grey and brown,
It makes me feel so frightfully down.
If you can help save the ocean and the land,
I'm sure we could all save everything, yes we can.
If I help, will you help?
Maybe the elephant seals can eat more kelp.

Bryony Steele-Perkins (9)
Milverton CP School, Taunton

Preserving Nature

The untouched, fresh, original woodland.
A river leaking crystal.
A mesmerising scene!

But . . . it is not hard to tell what will happen next
For any human being.

Preservation, education
We need this for nature.

Lily Cubitt (10)
Milverton CP School, Taunton

War Started

War started off as a bit of fun,
the English and the Germans playing with a gun.

Hitler was bad and started to fight,
as the bombs went off it gave us a fright.

It's really not good to take a life,
that's what we've learnt since 1945.

Jordan Morrod (9)
Milverton CP School, Taunton

Save Life

Earth being destroyed as more litter and waste
humans throw down!
Sea animals will go extinct
and waves will turn into wastelands!

We need to sustain the world
By not turning waves into waste lands,
We can reduce our carbon footprint by an amount!

Tyrone Tucker (10)
Milverton CP School, Taunton

Be Eco

A petrifying sight so horrible that it kills your eyes.
People are dying around the world because of us.
We're killing Mother Nature,
Destroying Planet Earth,
Wrecking the thing that God made.
If we don't do something now
More and more people are going to die.

Ben Maunder (8)
Milverton CP School, Taunton

Pollution

Pollution is bad,
The world is sad
Don't drop litter
Make things better
Litter is bitter
Do something good
And make the world a happier place to live.

Ethan May Wallace (9)
Milverton CP School, Taunton

Save Water

Drip drop, drip drop
Turn off the tap to save water
Drip drop, drip drop
Turn off the tap to help save the world
Drip drop, drip drop
Drip drop, drip drop, stop!

Matthew Lee (9)
Milverton CP School, Taunton

War

War makes me bored
People end up in wards
Nothing but pain
With all the bloodstain
All this bloodshed
Makes people dead.

Isaac Orszag-Land (9)
Milverton CP School, Taunton

Rubbish

Terrible, miserable and brown
Rubbish started to drown
I am disappointed in the human race
Show respect for the place
Don't dump rubbish in a stream
It makes animals want to scream.

Chloe Payne (9)
Milverton CP School, Taunton

Save The World!

I'm so amazed about what we're doing to the world
It is wicked and cruel
I'm feeling shattered
Some buildings are destroyed because of us
We can change this
Please help!

Cameron Stuart-Taylor (8)
Milverton CP School, Taunton

Don't Harm Them

Destroying the world day by day, killing animals.
Losing their homes for us to live our lives with no thought.
Lives are lost for their coats to keep us warm, stop.
Tigers are dying hour by hour thanks to mankind.
Tearful as they slowly fall to the ground breathless.
The beautiful creature that once roamed the world cannot anymore.

Brianna Whelan (10)
Milverton CP School, Taunton

Help Me

I don't deserve this, living in the cold with my three-year-old,
With other homeless people all around.
No shelter living out on the streets,
Soggy clothes when it's raining.
Waking up cold and damp from sleeping under cardboard,
What is the government doing to help?

Cameron Hodson (8)
Milverton CP School, Taunton

The Eco-Poem

Ice caps are melting
Floodwater destroying crops
Please turn off the lights
Save the world because it's dying
Turn down heating in the house.

Oscar Tickner (7)
Milverton CP School, Taunton

The Worse World

Murky waters lurking around dirty, flooded homes.
Young children wearing old, ruined clothes that itch very badly.
Poor polar bears losing polar ice caps because of global warming.
Pollution looking like mist when there is smog in other countries.
Bombed factory that is spooky and you think ghosts will fly out.

Maisy Crawford (8)
Milverton CP School, Taunton

Save The World

Dust storms cause trouble
Lots of polar bears have died
I feel worried, stop and think!
Please can you use Ecover?
Can you stop cutting down trees?

Jessica Gammon (7)
Milverton CP School, Taunton

The Eco-Poem

Horrified children
Everybody heartbroken
Power station smog
Pollution damaging Earth
Use your feet not cars.

Jesse Musson (7)
Milverton CP School, Taunton

Save The World

Littering rivers
The waste is killing our land
We all feel helpless
Loggers cutting rainforests
Horrified people homeless.

Oscar Sharman (7)
Milverton CP School, Taunton

When People Cut Down The Trees

When people cut down the trees, it makes animals flee.
They run away to find a place to stay until the day comes again.
Don't blame the men who cut down the trees, they do not get much money.
When people cut down the trees.

Hannah Thomas (9)
Milverton CP School, Taunton

Polar Bears

All the ice has melted away
Polar bears are hungry
The muddy lands they don't like
The polar bears feel sad, unhappy, scared and miserable,
We hope they will live.

Katie McMillan (8)
Milverton CP School, Taunton

Our Wonderful Planet Turns Bad

We need to think about our world.
If you don't reduce, reuse and recycle
You could pollute our world!
How would you feel if you were the planet?
All that electricity you use pollutes the planet!

Dionne Holmans-Price (8)
Milverton CP School, Taunton

Recycle For The Future

A plastic pool waiting for reinvention
Arriving from homes across the country.
Support the Earth, retain the planet.
Recycling for the future.
Holding onto the planet for our grandchildren.

Campbell Marriott (10)
Milverton CP School, Taunton

Pollution Damaging Earth!

Horrified children
Pollution damaging Earth
Greenhouse gas warming
Everybody's heartbroken
Flooding killing animals.

Douglas Landon (7)
Milverton CP School, Taunton

We Pollute The Air

Factories use gas
Polar bears need lots of ice
Everyone feels sad
The world is being destroyed
We need to save animals.

Ben Alford (7)
Milverton CP School, Taunton

The Eco-Poem

Polar bears need ice
Flood water destroying homes
It makes me feel sad
We are turning off the lights
We are turning off the taps.

Charles Blundell (8)
Milverton CP School, Taunton

The Pollution Rap

Open your eyes
Look into the skies
The clouds are going grey
And it may happen today
So look out and recycle
Look out for smoke
Factories are working
And they're killing our folk
Recycling is fun
Dumping is a bum
So don't put it in the bin
Put your rubbish in the recycling bin
And help the world to sing
Don't you care anymore?
Don't be a bore
Recycle and save the world
Then if you recycle
You'll have enough money
To buy a bicycle
And an expensive pearl
Yoghurts can be edible
Even after a week
Don't chuck your yoghurts away
Eat them quick
And don't waste food
It will be in the dump today.

Lyle Cann (10)
Sharpness Primary School, Berkeley

Stop Pollution

What are we doing to the Earth?
We're smothering the world with litter.
Our oxygen is full of toxic gases and chemicals.
Stamp out pollution!

Children are dying from drinking dirty water,
People dying from diseases every day.
Our world's vanishing,
Stop littering the Earth.
Stamp out pollution!

Your ignorance is stupid,
We can't stop it alone, we need your help.
Do you want to be a murderer?
Then stop pollution now.
We need to stop it!

Help the world,
We need to stop pollution,
We need to stop it now.
What are you going to do about it?

Joeley Heeps (9)
Sharpness Primary School, Berkeley

End Pollution Now

What in the world is going on?
All the damage you do is wrong.
The animals that live in the ponds and rivers
Are dead because of your pollution.

You are sacrificing the Earth,
All the toxic waste is smothering the country.
Our world was clean and smelt nice,
So stop it *now!*

Jasmine Atkinson (9)
Sharpness Primary School, Berkeley

Pollution

Does no one care what's happening?
The biggest killer is human.
You're tearing your home apart,
Bit by bit.
What do you think you're doing?
Finish it immediately!

Does no one care what's happening?
You're murdering the planet!
The planet is being our sacrifice.
Have you got a brain cell?
Is it minute?
Finish it immediately!

This is a destructive thing,
What are you going to do about it?
Become people of the human race.
What about the environment?
We should contribute to make it better.
Finish it immediately!

Dominic Brown (11)
Sharpness Primary School, Berkeley

Pollution

Does no one understand?
Our world's beginning to suffer
Our country is in danger
So stop it now!

Your pollution is making us worried
Who the Hell do you think you are?

You are making danger
And hurting living things.

Soon it will be you!

Robert Stevens (9)
Sharpness Primary School, Berkeley

Stop Pollution

Pollution is dreadful,
It makes me feel bad.
It gives me a hardened heart,
With the damage we are doing.
Aren't you all worried?

Our environment is turning to a living Hell.
Our world's being sacrificed,
For our own messy greediness.
My head is spinning,
The way people are refusing to stop it.
Is it you!

The children are all dying,
From the dirty, horrid water.
You're killing the Earth,
With all the sadness I am feeling.
Why are you doing it?
Stop it now.

Philippa Susan Harvey (10)
Sharpness Primary School, Berkeley

Stop Pollution

Does anyone know what is happening?
Do you think of the sadness that I feel?
Don't you care anymore?
Many more animals are dying,
So please recycle.
When will this craziness stop?
The pollution in this world by itself,
You have to help us.

Kieron Tyrrell (10)
Sharpness Primary School, Berkeley

Pollution Rap

Doesn't anyone care about the world?
All the damage that's going on,
Trains crashing at the speed of light.
Has your brain been minimised?
All the dead fish, all the toxic waste,
Schools being knocked down,
Animals dying, buildings knocked down,
Planes crashing in tragedy,
Save the animals' cubs,
Save the animals.

Save the human race,
But most of all
Save the whole world,
Otherwise you'll wish
You'd never been born.

Shae Smith (9)
Sharpness Primary School, Berkeley

Shattered World

Does no one understand
What's happened to our beautiful place
And to our land?
It's a terrible disgrace.

More and more people are getting this feeling,
We need to restore the world's power,
It's coming down from the ceiling,
It will happen in an hour.

Don't you care anymore
How people feel?
It's come to the floor,
This is so real.

Callum Thompson (10)
Sharpness Primary School, Berkeley

My Thought Of Pollution

What do you think you are doing?
You're wrecking the Earth, that's what you're doing.
We are drenching the Earth's flame,
Why are you extinguishing the Earth's flame?
The angels are rusting and the Earth
Is getting burnt by the human flame.
Our heavenly height is getting closer to Hell.
You are taking your last glance
At the world's existence.
Does the environment look like an illusion?
The Earth is turning into an overfull bin,
The woodlands are being conquered
By the human flame.
Now stop acting like you don't care,
And do something!

Thomas Cotton (11)
Sharpness Primary School, Berkeley

Pollution

The gloominess that I feel,
The less people you heel,
You are killing the sea animals,
Fish, dolphin, jellyfish, sharks and seals
And you still don't care,
Pollution be aware!

Do you know what you are doing?
You are being harmful to all the animals,
Drinking the water and having fun,
Just look around,
You are making them ill
And you never think first!

Leah Priday (10)
Sharpness Primary School, Berkeley

Stop Pollution Now

What is happening to our world?
What is going on?
Pollution smothers the towns and cities,
You're cruel to do this to the world.
Stop pollution *now!*

Help our world, it's crumbling away
You're just murderers
You're letting your ignorance stand in our way
Stop pollution *now!*

You're just greedy people searching for more power
You are criminals destroying the world
Why is your craziness overpowering you?
What are you going to do about it now?
Stop pollution!

Rachael Riley (9)
Sharpness Primary School, Berkeley

Pollution

Does no one understand,
What is happening to our world?
We are killing all the animals and the fish in the sea.
Do you know how much we are damaging our Earth?
The animals are being deprived of their world because of your laziness!
We're filling the streets and the seas with rubbish.
We are polluting the water, the water that comes out of our taps!
It is becoming limited,
Do you care?

Animals are the victims in all of this.
They are dying,
All because we can't be bothered to recycle our waste.
They are ill and we don't even care.
Stop it now!

Annie Allen (10)
Sharpness Primary School, Berkeley

Pollution

Do you not understand?
How small is your brain?
Innocent animals deprived of oxygen,
You're killing our world.

Walking, cycling; better than driving.
Taking a bus, taking the train, flying in a plane.
All equals the same -
Pollution.

Helpless children dying from drinking dirty, infected water,
When is this gonna stop?
It better be now!

Erin Smith (11)
Sharpness Primary School, Berkeley

Stop Pollution

What are you doing to this planet?
What's going on?
You're smothering the Earth with rubbish,
You're killing the animals,
Stop pollution!

Have you seen what you're doing?
Your laziness is killing the planet.
The diseases in the polluted water are killing the human race.
Stop pollution!

So what are you going to do about it?
Pick up the rubbish.

Charlotte Heeps (9)
Sharpness Primary School, Berkeley

Pollution

What have we done to our world?
Damaging our fish
Putting gas in the planet
Will it be the same in the future?
Or will it be worse?
Please stop this now before it's too late
Please don't ignore what's happened to our beautiful world
Help us to stop the pollution, *now!*

Kyran Edwards (9)
Sharpness Primary School, Berkeley

Stop Pollution

Your ignorance gets on my nerves
You've killed children
You've damaged our city
You've turned our world to pieces
You've killed our fish
Stop your craziness
You're a bunch of murderers.

Jobie Morris (9)
Sharpness Primary School, Berkeley

Pollution

What the hell is going on?
Stop all this craziness and start realising what is happening to our world,
Look what we have done to our world,
Is there a solution?
What are you going to do about it?

Tia Donna Paskin (9)
Sharpness Primary School, Berkeley

Cleaner And Greener

In a cleaner world I would see:
No stinky litter stacked up on the floor,
No precious food wasted,
No smelly dog poo piling on the pavements.

In a cleaner world I would see:
No poisonous pollution taking over the air.
Don't ever drive, take your bikes,
Alternatively walk.
The sparkling grass, clean and shiny.

In a cleaner world I would see:
Fragile habitats surviving every day,
The mighty ocean shining in the sun,
Dirty litterbugs destroyed.

In a greener world I would see:
Fresh green grass shining in the sun,
No horrible chemicals being poured into the sea,
No dangerous rubbish killing our animals.

In a greener world I would see:
No humungous flats being built,
No cute, fluffy animals being killed,
No killing other hopeless people.

Connor Smith (8)
Windwhistle Primary School, Weston-super-Mare

Keep Our World Clean!

Someone here has crashed a car
And left a burnt-through tyre.
If other vandals come along,
It might be set on fire.

Look at us and all the ducks
Drowning in pollution.
But some of us, like myself,
Want bigger resolutions!

So all look on the brighter side,
We'll simply clear it up!
Do you want to join us
In our Save the World club?

Now loads of wild flowers decorate
The steep and grassy bank,
Along the crystal rhyne,
The ducks are quacking out
Their thanks!

Several happy families
Picnic by the rhyne.
Come on everybody, help
To keep our world clean!

Tamsin Sayers (8)
Windwhistle Primary School, Weston-super-Mare

The Evergreen Rhyne

Apples red, apples green,
Sadly bobbing in the rhyne.
Shattered glass glints and shines,
Bright as children's eager eyes.

A rubbish jumble in full view,
Nothing neat, nothing new.
Water brushes littered sides
And weaves among the filth it hides.

An old and rusty can of Coke,
It must be thrown by careless folk.
Whoever threw the red ball
Must have really been a fool.

Flocks of ducks upon the rhyne,
Everything is fresh and green.
Clean and green is very nice,
So here's some serious advice.

Throw in crumbs of lovely bread,
But not a can or broken bed.
Remember everything was bitter
Back when we had heaps of litter.

George Shortman (8)
Windwhistle Primary School, Weston-super-Mare

Help!

The rhyne is browner and duller every day.
There are no daisies to make daisy-chains,
No flowers and no honey for us.
Why don't people use their brains?

There are crazy people throwing glasses.
They throw them in the streets and streams.
They tip out truck-loads of rubbish
And ruin the flower banks of the rhyne.

Rubber gloves are sticking in mud,
Forgotten bottles bob in the weeds.
Flattened footballs are soft and sad,
With broken dolls among the reeds.

We need to help our local town,
We want to keep it cleaner.
We need to save our animals.
We want our world greener.

Bethany Bevan-Edwards (8)
Windwhistle Primary School, Weston-super-Mare

Rubbish In The Rhyne

Brown and disgusting,
Lost balls hover in the Rhyne's filthy soup;
Crushed cans brighten the duckweed
Like horrible flowers;
Colourful, ripped packets of crisps
Float where a rubbery glove drifts.

Filthy footballs in the Rhyne,
Not good for ducky 'eating machines'!
The ducks will die
And so will we,
So that's why we must keep them free!

Scott Ferguson (8)
Windwhistle Primary School, Weston-super-Mare

After The Clean-Up

The tiny stream comes rushing through
The tunnel of the bridge,
Where ducks are quacking happily
And drifting gracefully by.

Cheerful picnickers dip their toes
In the cool, clean water,
Splashing them back and forth
On a hot summer's day.

Men and boys are fishing,
Catching hoards of silver treasure.
Little girls are breaking bread
And throwing crumbs to the bobbing ducks.

The sun reflects off the gleaming river.
I wish it could stay this clean forever!

Courtney Barnett (8)
Windwhistle Primary School, Weston-super-Mare

A Cleaner World

In a cleaner world you would see:
Multicoloured leaves that never
Fall off in the autumn and in the winter.
Shiny, clear waters,
In the water there will be
Beautiful rainbow fish in different sizes.
Blue and grey dolphins in the
Clean blue sea on the hottest day.

You would see:
The hot beach with coconut palms and palm trees,
Violet flowers in the wonderful meadow,
The biggest trees, like a giraffe with
Lots of yellow, green and red leaves.

Xena Vincent-Major
Windwhistle Primary School, Weston-super-Mare

Help To Clean The Rhyne

Dirty, crawling, creeping litter
Giving the Rhyne a slow, nasty death.
The crystal water has turned to slime
And the breeze has got a stinking breath.

Flocks of tissue paper block the view
Of the shadowy mirror below,
With people chucking rubbish around
It is stopping the timid flowers grow.

The ducks are sadly drifting down
The scum of the litter-piled river.
We need to spend time cleaning the Rhyne
So ducks and people can live here forever.

Chloe Turnbull
Windwhistle Primary School, Weston-super-Mare

A Cleaner World

In a cleaner world you would see:
Soft, clean animals,
A cleaner pond where fish and ducks can swim,
No more tree-cutting because of habitats.

You would see:
No more litterbugs,
No more dumping in rivers,
A family of dolphins swimming in the crystal sea.

You would see:
Mother Nature carrying on life,
Fresh air without smoky air from factories,
Build more habitats for reptiles and others.

Jordan Clark (8)
Windwhistle Primary School, Weston-super-Mare

Go Green

In a greener world we would see:
Sparkling grass like a helicopter shining through the air,
Twinkling sky with the bluest and whitest clouds,
Twinkling sky with the bluest water ever.

In a greener world we would see:
Nice hot beaches with no rubbish in sight,
Children playing nicely in the soft grass,
With no rubbish in sight,
Crystal-clear water with no pollution,
Cans or cigarette ends floating like small boats.

Brooklyn Sheppard
Windwhistle Primary School, Weston-super-Mare

A Cleaner World

In a cleaner world you would see:
Golden, soft sands like a collar around the coastline,
Rainbow fish swimming deep into the blue waves,
Bright light twinkling on petals of a beautiful flower in autumn.

You would see:
Rolling hills of the sweetest grass stretching as far as the eye can see,
Crystal-clear seas sparkling through the sunlight.
In a bright blue sky, seagulls;
And people breathing in the cleanest air.

Jack Anelay (8)
Windwhistle Primary School, Weston-super-Mare

A Cleaner World

In a cleaner world you will see:
Colourful houses which are beautiful.
Leaping, colourful fish diving in a rich blue sea.
The sweet-smelling grass.

You would see:
Warm, soft, golden sand
With an inviting blue sea,
A fresh, clean world,
Happy, smiling children.

Craig Feltham
Windwhistle Primary School, Weston-super-Mare

A Cleaner And Greener World

In a cleaner world I would see:
Sparkling green grass waving in the wind,
All schools working together to keep the children safe,
We would not see dirty litter creeping down the road.

In a greener world I would see:
No litter hiding in the rhyne,
No dirty water flowing down the stream,
No dangerous and disgusting smoking,
It makes people die.

Trudy Thomas (8)
Windwhistle Primary School, Weston-super-Mare

A Cleaner World

In a cleaner world you would see:
Sparkling blue sea where fish can swim,
No rubbish on the floor,
More flowers getting planted
As the sun gets hotter and hotter.

You would see:
More ducks coming out to swim,
Fresh, clean air where birds can fly and sing sweetly,
Crystal mountains, blue and white.

Shauni Kibby
Windwhistle Primary School, Weston-super-Mare

A Cleaner World

In a cleaner world you would see:
Rivers that sparkle like medals,
Forests that gleam like crystals,
The greenest and cleanest grass imaginable.

You would see:
Litter-free golden sands,
White, shiny glaciers that don't melt,
The healthiest corals swaying in the sea.

Rhys Williams (8)
Windwhistle Primary School, Weston-super-Mare

A Cleaner World

In a cleaner world you would see:
No more pollution in the air,
Cars using less petrol,
Birds flying in the air.

You would see:
Less pollution from factories,
Less traffic and people walking,
Less towns because it gets busy.

Joshua Honeyman (8)
Windwhistle Primary School, Weston-super-Mare

In A Cleaner And Greener World

In a cleaner and greener world I would see:
No precious food wasted on the floor,
No creepy litter sneaking along the ground,
No beautiful animals dying.

In a greener world I would see:
No horrible litter hiding in the bushes,
No dangerous rubbish killing our animals.
No horrible and nasty homes being built.

James Tanner (8)
Windwhistle Primary School, Weston-super-Mare

In A Cleaner And Greener World

In a cleaner world I would see:
No filthy litter hiding in the bushes,
No dangerous cigarettes trying to harm people,
No disgusting water making children ill.

In a cleaner and greener world:
No nasty houses being built,
People clean up the dog poo,
Fresh grass shining in the sun.

Sophie Brooks (8)
Windwhistle Primary School, Weston-super-Mare

A Cleaner And Greener World

In a cleaner world I would see:
No smelly litter piling up,
Shiny blue water swishing on the beach,
No dangerous pollution spreading in the world.

In a greener world I would see:
Fresh, clean air spreading in the lovely sky,
No stinky, dirty cigarettes piling on the floor,
No disgusting black water being drunk by innocent people.

Ryan Pickles (8)
Windwhistle Primary School, Weston-super-Mare

A Cleaner And Greener World

In a cleaner world I would see:
Fragile energy being used sensibly,
Stinky litter scraping across the floor,
No precious animals going extinct.

In a greener world I would see:
No dangerous bags killing Earth's animals,
No dirty chemicals being poured into the sea,
No nasty fires destroying important buildings.

Drew Cotterell (8)
Windwhistle Primary School, Weston-super-Mare

A Cleaner World

In a cleaner world you would see:
Shiny, colourful grass swaying gracefully in the breeze,
Birds singing sweetly in the trees,
Fresh, clean air without any pollution.

You would see . . .
Colourful roses sprouting from their buds,
Greenest mountains with a crystal clear
View of the countryside.

Connor Read
Windwhistle Primary School, Weston-super-Mare

A Cleaner And Greener World

In a cleaner world I would see:
Less cars and more people walking.
I wouldn't see horrible chemicals being poured into the sea.
There would not be any leftovers for disgusting rats to eat.

In a greener world I would see:
No more diseased rats.
I would see more fresh water.
I would not see any more hunting animals.

Anthony Hamer (9)
Windwhistle Primary School, Weston-super-Mare

A Cleaner And Greener World

In a cleaner world we would see:
Sparkly green grass sprouting from the ground,
Mighty plants growing in the ground,
Safe water surviving in the taps.

In a greener world we would see:
No disgusting litter floating across the sea,
No filthy carrier bags hiding in the sea,
No smelly litter creeping across the floor.

Ella-May Matthews (8)
Windwhistle Primary School, Weston-super-Mare

Message From The Rhyne

Scrambles of rubbish stuck in hedges,
Tangles of rubbish line the edges,
A watery sludge of creeping litter,
Where revolting water's dark and bitter.

People chuck in apples and trikes,
Shattered ladders and broken bikes,
A rubber glove, like a drowning hand,
Is a warning that people should understand!

Ronan Jennens
Windwhistle Primary School, Weston-super-Mare

A Cleaner World

In a cleaner world you would see:
Cleaner air around the world,
Huge forests giving habitats to thousands of creatures,
Caring people looking after friends, family and neighbours.

You would see:
Blue sky, completely clean,
Mountains with the whitest snow,
Golden sand shining like the sun.

Shane Lemm (8)
Windwhistle Primary School, Weston-super-Mare

A Cleaner World

In a cleaner world you would see:
Caring people looking after friends, family and neighbours,
Huge forests providing habitats for countless exotic animals,
Clean oceans full of beautiful rainbow fish.

You would see:
White icebergs which haven't melted,
Water as blue as the sky,
The most beautiful noise of birds.

Samantha Mansell (8)
Windwhistle Primary School, Weston-super-Mare

Making A Difference In the World

Do not cut down trees
Because they give us oxygen.
You might take homes of animals
That live in high trees.
The world might not last.
The environment is dying,
Animals do die
Because of the tools used
To cut down the high trees.
Do not throw your litter,
You need to start recycling,
Running out of space,
We haven't got much space to live.
Do not waste water,
Because we are running out of it.
Walk to school a lot,
Do not use petrol power.

Robert Dent (9)
Withington CE Primary School, Cheltenham

Saving The World!

S aving the world is hard
A bag could kill a bird
V alue the world
I n the world you need to look after animals
N ever throw away rubbish on the floor
G etting the world back together

T hrow away food peelings in the compost heap
H elp the world
E arth is good to us

W ell it is a good world
O ne planet
R ich people throw away more paper
L ovely home
D o you recycle paper? You should.

Charlotte Furniss (8)
Withington CE Primary School, Cheltenham

Save The World And Keep It Clean

R efill your recycling bins with plastic bottles
E mpty plastic bags can be reused or recycled
C ardboard can be sent off to the recycling plant or used
for school models
Y ou could recycle and they could be reused again, over and over
C ut your pieces of paper then put them in the recycling bin
L ittle paper bags, you can keep them for toys or pens
E verything plastic can be reused.

Jordan Taylor (9)
Withington CE Primary School, Cheltenham

Making A Difference In The Word

S aving the town by recycling
A good recycling of the city
V isit a recycling centre
I am reusing plastic bags
N ow I am recycle a bag to put rubbish in
G et to the centre and see the recycling man

T he world needs to be recycling
H elp by always putting rubbish in the recycling bins
E veryone has recycling bins to put rubbish in

W ith rubbish, everyone needs to put it in the recycling
O n the recycling day, the people don't forget
R euse a bike
L eft rubbish on the floor
D ads always eat food and put it in the bin.

Kyran Pinchin (9)
Withington CE Primary School, Cheltenham

Recycle More

R euse your own shopping bags
E arth is getting smaller each day
C onservation is good for the planet
Y ou can use less bags
C utting trees will hurt animals
L iving animals die each day
E ach day we produce 50% of rubbish -
why not throw less away?

Daniel Phillips (8)
Withington CE Primary School, Cheltenham

Don't Throw More Rubbish Away

R ubbish can be recycled at recycling centres
E verybody can take it to the rubbish dump
C an you put the rubbish in the recycling bins?
Y ou can take the rubbish to the dump with all the rubbish
C an you help more people by recycling more?
L ater you can take rubbish to the recycling centres
E very day people recycle more paper and cans.

Ebony Odore (9)
Withington CE Primary School, Cheltenham

Young Writers Information

We hope you have enjoyed reading this book - and that you will continue to enjoy it in the coming years.

If you like reading and writing poetry drop us a line, or give us a call, and we'll send you a free information pack.

Alternatively if you would like to order further copies of this book or any of our other titles, then please give us a call or log onto our website at www.youngwriters.co.uk

Young Writers Information
Remus House
Coltsfoot Drive
Peterborough
PE2 9JX
(01733) 890066